D0469731

THE *THINKING CLEARLY* SERIES
Series editor: Clive Calver

The *Thinking Clearly* series sets out the main issues in a variety of important subjects. Written from a mainstream Christian standpoint, the series combines clear biblical teaching with up-to-date scholarship. Each of the contributors is an authority in his or her field. The series is written in straightforward everyday language, and each volume includes a range of practical applications and guidance for further reading.

The series has two main aims:
1. To help Christians understand their faith better.
2. To show how Christian truths can illuminate matters of crucial importance in our society.

OMF International works in most East Asian countries, and among East Asian peoples around the world. It was founded by James Hudson Taylor in 1865 as the China Inland Mission. Our purpose is to glorify God through the urgent evangelisation of East Asia's billions.

In line with this, OMF Publishing seeks to motivate and equip Christians to make disciples of all peoples. Publications include:

- stories and biographies showing God at work in East Asia
- the biblical basis of mission and mission issues
- the growth and development of the church in Asia
- studies of Asian culture and religion

Books, booklets, articles and free downloads can be found on our web at *www.omf.org*

Addresses for OMF English-speaking centres can be found at the back of this book.

THE *THINKING CLEARLY* SERIES

Series editor: Clive Calver

The Great Commission

ROSE DOWSETT

MONARCH
BOOKS

Mill Hill, London & Grand Rapids, Michigan

First published by Monarch Books in the UK in 2001,
Concorde House, Grenville Place,
Mill Hill, London, NW7 3SA.

Published in the USA by Monarch Books 2001.

Distributed by:
UK: STL, PO Box 300, Kingstown Broadway, Carlisle,
Cumbria CA3 0QS;
USA: Kregel Publications, PO Box 2607,
Grand Rapids, Michigan 49501.

ISBN 1 85424 515 5 (UK)
ISBN 0 8254 6032 8 (USA)

British Library Cataloguing Data
A catalogue record for this book is available
from the British Library.

Book design and production for the publishers by
Bookprint Creative Services
P.O. Box 827, BN21 3YJ, England
Printed in Great Britain.

Contents

Preface

I lay in a downtown Manila hospital, critically ill and drifting in and out of consciousness. The doctor caring for me expected me to die, and had told me so. A devout Christian man, his great concern was that I should have made my peace with God – and indeed with anybody else with whom I might have unsettled business. He prayed beside my bed with grace and compassion. My unconsciousness deepened.

People came and went, speaking to each other about me, wondering how long I would live. I could not respond to them, or even indicate how much I heard. But deep down inside my being, another conversation was going on, between myself and God. "Lord, this is such an expensive way to have a funeral! If I was going to die, why didn't you just let it happen back home six months ago?" "My child, will you trust me?" came the gentle reply. "Alright, Lord. I do trust you. But, did I get it all wrong, coming here to be a missionary?" "No, child, you didn't get it wrong. But, tell me: do you love me even more than you love what you think you can do for me?" A long pause. "Lord, I truly want to love you above all else. And I truly want to trust you absolutely."

A couple of weeks later, to everyone's surprise, including my own, I emerged from coma into the long, hard and erratic process of recovery. It was to be many months before I could even begin to cope with everyday life. To this day, I carry in my body the consequences of such severe illness.

Yet, profound though the impact on my body was, the impact in other ways was deeper still. I came to the conviction, steadily reinforced through my reading of Scripture down through the years, that however important the task, more important still is the living God from whom the task flows. I discovered in new ways how crucial, and how beautiful, it is for passion for the Lord and passion for his truth to come together. I realised how much I had yet to learn, about trusting God in circumstances I would not have chosen, and in many other ways as well. In my acute weakness – I was very ill in a strange country to which I had only recently come, newly married to a husband who was himself convalescent, unable to speak the local languages – it was those I had "come to help" who cared for me, pouring out love and every kind of practical service on this foreigner in their midst. It transformed and defined my relationships with Filipino colleagues and changed my understanding of missionary service in many significant ways.

And, yes, it made me think much more deeply about the Great Commission. I had come to Christian faith at the age of seventeen through reading the New Testament from cover to cover three times in three weeks. I had set out to disprove it, and instead found myself gripped by the person at the heart of it, the Lord Jesus Christ. The institutional church, it had seemed to me, deserved only scorn: was it not sickeningly hypocritical, over and over again the cause of war and violence and oppression? Yet here in the pages of Scripture, the calling of God's people to stand at the frontier between faith and unbelief, and to live out dynamically the love and grace of God, leapt out at me. How could anyone who claimed to take the Christian message seriously not then devote his or her life to urging it upon others? I could not divorce discipleship from mission. I had been born into a worldwide family, with global privileges but also global responsibilities. I could not have the one without the other. So, from the very start of my Christian life, the Great Commission was central. Within weeks, by a strange series of events, I was sure that one day the Lord would take me to Asia as a missionary. The task might be enormous, but it was surely inescapable.

Nothing that happened during the next few years, including family tragedy, family opposition, and the options opened up after university, shook that conviction, though it was tested to the limit. On the contrary, I became increasingly certain that God was asking me to invest my life in world mission. So, it was no surprise to find myself in Asia, arriving on my twenty-sixth birthday in Singapore, en route to the Philippines, where my fiancé was already working. But it *was* a surprise, a few brief months later, apparently to be dying, with the task that I thought I was about to begin instead already completed, at least as far as I was concerned.

And then, that deep-down conversation with the Lord, as vivid, as immediate, as indelible as any exchange could ever be. That haunting, penetrating question: "Tell me: do you love me even more than you love what you think you can do for me?"

And so, in the more than thirty years since then, my life, and that of my husband, has indeed been invested in world mission. It has often worked out far differently from what we could ever have imagined, and we were only able to live in Asia for eight brief though life-changing years. We still believe, passionately, that the whole world needs to hear the good news about Jesus Christ. But I also believe that first of all our focus needs to be on the one who gives the task. The Great Commission is then rooted not primarily in a few verses, a few commands, at the ends of the Gospels, but rather in the glorious character of God himself, utterly consistent through time and eternity. The focus is not primarily on what we do, but on who God is.

It is my prayer that this will be a liberating truth to those who read this book, and that as we try to think more clearly about the Great Commission we shall be inspired both to love the Lord more dearly and to engage in mission with glad and open hearts.

PART I

Thinking Clearly about the Great Commission

1

The Last Word

The last words of the risen Lord Jesus before his ascension into heaven must have shaken his disciples to the core. Two thousand years later, if we take them seriously, they still both shock us and thrill us. In this chapter, we begin to explore their meaning.

The Last Word

Your attitude should be the same as that of Christ Jesus:
Who, being in very nature God,
did not consider equality with God
something to be grasped,
but made himself nothing,
taking the very nature of a servant,
being made in human likeness.
And being found in appearance as a man,
he humbled himself
and became obedient to
death – even death on a cross!
Therefore God exalted him to the highest place
and gave him the name that is above every name,
that at the name of Jesus every knee should bow,
in heaven and on earth and under the earth,
and every tongue confess that Jesus Christ is Lord,
to the glory of God the Father.

Philippians 2:5–11

"If you hold to my teaching, you are really my disciples."

John 8:31

God has appointed Christ to be the heir of the world in his kingdom of grace, and to possess and reign over all nations, through the propagation of his gospel, and the power of his Spirit communicating the blessing of it.

Jonathan Edwards (1703–1757)

To be a Christian is to be a member of a missionary community and to become a participant in the activity of a missionary God.

Daniel Niles (1908–1970)

Discipleship must always be discipleship-in-movement-to-the-world. The disciple who will not lay down his life for the world and for the gospel of reconciliation is not worthy of being a follower of Jesus Christ.

Charles Van Engen

When I first became a Christian, I was very self-centred about it. It was great to feel forgiven and loved, to have someone to turn to and ask for things. Looking back, I don't think I really had much of a clue. I suppose it's a bit like being a newborn baby: something momentous has happened, but you've still got everything to learn. But gradually the penny dropped. As I got to know God better, and realised more and more what an amazing Being he is, I wanted to love him for himself, not just for what I could get out of him. And then, of course, I found I wanted to tell other people about him, and see them put their whole lives in his hands, where they belong. That's what being a disciple is all about, isn't it?

A Scottish student

A never-to-be-forgotten day

Imagine the scene. Eleven men had gathered on an unnamed mountainside, in the north of Palestine. They had trudged the best part of a hundred miles from Jerusalem. They were emotionally exhausted. Who wouldn't be, after all they had been through in a few short weeks? They had experienced the heights of giddy hope and the depths of crushing despair, not once but over and over again. They had lived for weeks in fear of their lives. They had endured the spine-tingling shock of having their best friend and inspirational leader publicly executed, and then eerily, unbelievably, break free from a heavily guarded rock tomb and appear among them on several distinct occasions. They had invested three years of their lives, at great cost, in a dream and a cause, and now it seemed as if it had all come crashing down around their ears.

Or had it? Had the incredible events of the past few days opened a chink of light for the future? Could they dare to hope – something, anything? Little fragments of what they had been told but not properly grasped at the time kept drifting back to their minds. Could the unthinkable be actually happening, in ways they could never have foreseen? Was God truly among them in dramatic grace, bringing to fulfilment the promises of centuries? Did they dare believe that, or would that lead them only to greater pain and danger and betrayal all over again? How confused and frightened they must have been.

And then, their familiar leader was suddenly back among them. At least, he was recognisable, but not exactly the same as the man with whom they had travelled the length and breadth of their country: the one who had sat in their boats and slept in their homes, who had healed the sick and fed the hungry and earned the implacable hatred of the religious leaders of the day, the one who had taught so clearly and simply and yet sometimes in incomprehensible riddles. Dearly familiar he might be, but there was also an awesome difference, for here was the one who had come back from the dead. Here was Jesus, and here were they, at this breath-taking moment which would shape the rest of their lives. Was this the end, or the beginning?

In that moment, the die was cast. It was the beginning. Only the start of the beginning, to be sure, but nonetheless a pivotal beginning, as men who had walked with Jesus as followers of a leader became worshippers of God among them, Emmanuel, "God with us". With painful honesty Matthew tells us that even then "some doubted"; whether because they mistrusted their senses, thought they must be seeing a ghost, or simply could not accept that the Messiah could be crucified, we are not told. But the transition had been made. Companions had become worshippers.

A never-to-be-forgotten mandate

It is in this highly charged context that the Lord Jesus gives the disciples his final instructions. For centuries, the church has known the concluding verses of Matthew's Gospel as "the Great Commission", in the same way that Matthew 22:37–39 is known as "the Great Commandment". There are variant versions in the other Gospels and at the beginning of Acts, but it is to Matthew's version that we most naturally turn whenever we think of the Great Commission.

What exactly is it that Jesus chooses to tell his disciples?

> Then Jesus came to them and said, "All authority in heaven and on earth has been given to me. Therefore go and make disciples of all nations, baptising them in the name of the Father and of the Son and of the Holy Spirit, and teaching them to obey everything I have commanded you. And surely I am with you always, to the very end of the age." (Matthew 28:18–20)

In fact, there is only one command in these verses: "make disciples of all nations". But, that command is encircled on the one hand by a breathtaking statement of fact ("all authority in heaven and earth has been given to me") and on the other by a comprehensive promise ("and surely I am with you always, to the very end of the age"), and explained by three activities ("as you go", "baptising", "teaching").

Jesus' claim to authority is sweeping. There is neither place nor time, nor even heaven or eternity, which falls outside it. It has been given, not seized. It is the authority of one who is equal in status with both Father and Holy Spirit, in other words fully God. No wonder he can make such a promise. He is Lord of the universe, and King of eternity. In the three years of his public ministry, Jesus has been saying, "Look! This is what the reign of God looks like. Now you go and do it and live it, too!" Because he is King, he delegates to his subjects the responsibility of demonstrating and explaining life in his kingdom. And, because he is King, he has both the right to do that, and the power to make it happen. For the time being, we may not see the King with our physical sight, though his promise is to be truly present even if invisible. But, when God's servants live the way we are called to live, then onlookers should be able to look on and say, "Ah, now we can see what living under God's rule is all about – and what kind of king God is".

The very idea that a mere eleven men, who up till then had not shown themselves to be especially reliable either in understanding or in faithfulness, should "make disciples of all nations", is absolutely preposterous. It must rank as one of the most lunatic commands of all time. Yet, set it within the context of the statement and the promise, and suddenly it halts you in your tracks. And that's exactly what happened to those first disciples. The task on its own, and out of context, was insane; but in the light of the Lord's authority and promise, it became their way of life. Without demur, they returned to Jerusalem to wait for the promised Holy Spirit. When he came, at Pentecost, they knew exactly what they were empowered to do, and they did it. They discipled the nations. First they discipled the Jews and proselytes of the Dispersion, gathered in Jerusalem from the far corners of the Roman Empire and beyond to celebrate Passover and Pentecost, those great festivals of the Jewish people; and then, through these men and women as they finally returned home, and also through direct apostolic activity, they reached out to the Gentile world beyond.

Going, baptising and teaching

Although "make disciples" is the only imperative in the Greek, Matthew makes it clear that there are inescapable tasks to undertake in order to fulfil the command. Perhaps "going, baptising and teaching" are illustrative rather than saying all there is to say. Or perhaps, each embraces a significant portion of what is involved in making disciples.

Going

Take "going". In the Old Testament, there is often a call to the nations to "come" to Jerusalem, to come to the Temple. There was even a special part of the Temple set aside for them, the Court of the Gentiles, where Jews were supposed to pray for Gentiles to come to faith in the one true God, and where Gentiles were supposed to be welcomed and instructed in the truth. Sadly, the Jews had lost sight of the purpose for which that part of the Temple had been built, and in any case most did not believe that God had anything in store for Gentiles except destruction. By the time of Jesus they had made the Court of the Gentiles the marketplace where the moneychangers and vendors of birds and animals for sacrifice carried out their business and cheated vulnerable pilgrims. It was this that made the Lord Jesus so angry on the famous occasion when he drove the moneychangers and exploitative traders from the Temple (Matthew 21:12ff).

Why had God wanted Gentiles to come to the Temple? Because it should be there, more than anywhere else, that they could find out about the one true and living God. It should be there that they could see the visual aids of sacrifice, and hear of the need for atonement for sin. It should be there that they could hear teaching from the Old Testament writings, and learn to sing the psalms, the songs of faith. It should be among God's people that outsiders would see the dynamic of living for God being worked out in families and in the whole community. Isaiah has a vision (cf Isaiah chapter 2) of the nations of the world flowing up to Jerusalem, bringing their worship and their gifts and their tribute. That would be glory indeed! Tragically, over the centuries it would seem that rather few Gentiles were welcomed and brought to faith as they visited Jerusalem.

But now, instead of having the nations come to God's people, the direction changes. Jesus' disciples are to go to the nations. The death and resurrection of the Lord Jesus meant that the sacrificial system, always only a visual aid pointing to the ultimate reality behind, was no longer needed. Jesus' sacrifice of himself was once and for all, complete and final. No longer was there any need for an altar, or even for the Temple. As Jesus died, the great heavy curtain that shut off the innermost part of the Temple had split from top to bottom, dramatically showing how now there is a new living way, open to all, into reconciliation with God. And the coming of the Holy Spirit meant that wherever God's people went, the Spirit who makes his home within them went with them. Wherever the disciples went – about their daily business, in their homes and neighbourhoods, or on intentional journeys to spread the message – they could take the good news of the Cross, and be empowered by the life-giving Spirit, and so "disciple the nations". "As you go," says Jesus, "wherever you go, make disciples."

Baptising

Down through the centuries, there have been many arguments about baptism, usually about who is eligible and at what age, about how much water must be used, and about who is qualified to administer it. Sadly, those arguments have often diverted attention from the simple and central significance of baptism.

When Jesus instructed the eleven disciples to baptise as an intrinsic part of making disciples, what did he mean? Baptism, of course, was not an exclusively Christian ritual. Nor did it begin in Jewish circles only with John the Baptist. It was practised by various Jewish sects, with varying significance. It appeared then, and appears now, in a variety of forms, in both pagan and other religious rituals. Generically, it seems to symbolise purification on the one hand (water washes away dirt) and initiation on the other (the water represents death, so that you go in as one person and emerge as another). Where the emphasis is on initiation, a person undergoes it only once. Where the emphasis is on purification, a person might undergo it repeatedly.

In John the Baptist's ministry, the appeal was to Jews to be baptised as an expression of repentance, recognising the awesome judgement of God on sin and their desperate need for grace and forgiveness. This, of course, was outrageous to many Jews, who believed that the very fact of being descended from Abraham gave them immunity from the wrath of God. But John's message resonated with many ordinary people, whatever their religious leaders might say. They wanted something more real than what they had already. In coming to John for baptism, they were expressing their desire to be on a different footing with God. They were also expressing their commitment to live from then on in a different way from in the past, in the light of God's demands. There was a recognition that God's people together were called to live in a manner that demonstrated God's intentions. John pointed forward to the one who was coming, Jesus, who would baptise not simply with the outward symbol of water but more profoundly with the Spirit who would purify inwardly and initiate into a new empowered way of life, dedicated to the service of God.

This, of course, is precisely what happened at Pentecost, when the Holy Spirit, promised by Jesus, came to "indwell" (live in and among) God's people. The disciples are filled with the Spirit, and immediately become God's mouthpiece among the crowds, gathered in Jerusalem from "every nation under heaven" (Acts 2:5). As Peter preaches his heart out, God is powerfully and most graciously at work. Some three thousand people express repentance and their desire for forgiveness of their sins through baptism in the name of Jesus Christ, receive the gift of the Holy Spirit, and so are initiated into the fledgling Christian community.

It is this fledgling community which is to be the place where men and women, boys and girls, are to be discipled. For this is the community which is called to be the dynamic expression of the character of God: Father, Son and Holy Spirit. It is a family, transcending biological families, sharing one heavenly Father. It is a redeemed community, sharing salvation from sin and judgement through the one and only Saviour, Jesus Christ. It is an organic community, brought into being and continuously being sustained by the Holy Spirit. Those within this community are to live out the new way of life into which they have been initiated, so that those outside may look on and see who the true and living God is: Creator, Father, Saviour, Judge and Life-giver.

Teaching

If baptism marks a beginning, it is only a beginning! No wonder the Lord Jesus includes "teaching them to obey everything I have commanded you" in the task of making disciples. It is important to realise that the Great Commission is not just about urging people to "decide to accept Christ", nor about being content to have people baptised, significant though both of these are. Initiation must be followed by progressive and radical change. A disciple is one who engages in an ongoing, close, learning relationship with his teacher. Discipleship involves faithful commitment through thick and thin.

Discipleship does not happen automatically or by accident. Just as a person needs to be nurtured and cared for through infancy and childhood, so a new Christian believer needs to be nurtured and cared for in order to grow into healthy adulthood. Nor do we ever grow out of the need for nurture and care, even though we may simultaneously be both nurturers and nurtured, care-givers and cared-for, because Jesus' disciples are to be formed into communities of people with interlocked and interdependent lives. The Great Commission does not say, "Watch people from all nations become disciples" or even, "Make sure that people from all nations become disciples". The command is very active! On the one hand, we are to be disciples of Jesus himself, not of some other person, however impressive a Christian leader he or she might be. On the other, the Lord is clearly instructing the Eleven to be directly instrumental in transforming people into disciples, life-long learners, those who are being progressively shaped by Jesus' teaching.

So, the starting point of initiation is to be complemented by ongoing teaching. Moreover, the teaching is to be thoroughly comprehensive, embracing personal and community life, relationship to God and to other people, attitudes, values and deeds, faith for the whole of life. Such was what Jesus had himself taught. Perhaps even more significantly here, this is three-dimensional teaching: teaching not only by word, but lived out in active personal and communal demonstration. It is at every level and in every form: one-to-one, in groups, in crowds; formal and informal; occasional and sustained; in official places of worship, in homes, in workplaces. Further, this is no casual pooling of ideas or tentative suggestion: Jesus' teaching is to be received and *obeyed*. The task of making disciples revolves around training in *obeying* Jesus' teaching.

Clearly, this is no "been there, done that" kind of agenda. When could you ever say that a nation, or even a person or small group, had been discipled as a totally completed task, with no more to be learned or taught, nothing more to be obeyed? What the Lord is describing here is breath-taking, not only in geographical and demographic extent, but also in scope and depth.

It is hard to imagine how that little band of men felt as they made their way back from Galilee to Jerusalem. At one level, nothing had changed. They were still a small, strangely assorted company of ex-fishermen and artisans, who had recently lived through deep trauma. They were still caught up in adjusting their dreams and hopes and expectations, still coming to terms with their leader's absence, still terrifyingly vulnerable to the violence and hatred of those who had so recently crucified their Lord. And yet, at another level, they weren't the same at all. Not only had they been transformed from followers into worshippers, they had also been entrusted with the most amazing mandate to change the world. Did they walk their several days' journey in stunned silence or in animated planning? Did they wonder how in the world they would do what they had been told to do? Did they simply hang on to that breath-taking statement – their Lord Jesus had all authority in heaven and on earth – and the equally breath-taking promise, that he would be with them every step of the way, whether or not they could see him with their physical eyes?

However it was, the significance of that encounter with the risen Christ has reverberated down through the years of history ever since.

Questions

1. Imagine yourself to be one of the Eleven, walking back to Jerusalem after Jesus' ascension. What do you think you would have talked about? How would you have felt about Jesus' instruction? Now imagine yourself to be one of the disciples immediately following Pentecost. How would this have transformed your response to the Great Commission?

2. In what ways do you as an individual, and the Christian community to which you belong, disciple others "as you go" about each day's business? What might going, baptising and teaching mean in practice for you today?

3. The Lord Jesus states that there is no person, and no place,

outside his eternal authority. How should that affect our relationships with unbelievers, and with often anti-Christian cultures?

4. How can we keep "growing" as disciples, and as disciple-makers, all our lives long?

2

Faith at the Frontiers

Was the Great Commission a particular command given only to the original Apostles, a unique word for a unique moment? Or is it a particular "re-casting" of a pervasive message of the Bible? In this chapter we set the Great Commission in the context of the whole Gospel of Matthew, and of the Old Testament.

Faith at the Frontiers

Mission work does not arise from any arrogance in the Christian Church: mission is its cause and its life. The Church exists by mission, just as fire exists by burning.

Emil Brunner (1889–1965)

There is no participation in Christ without participation in His mission to the world. That by which the Church receives its existence is that by which it is also given its world mission.

International Missionary Council at Willingen, Germany, 1952

And God spoke . . .: "You shall have no other gods before me. You shall not make for yourself an idol in the form of anything in heaven above or on the earth beneath or in the waters below. You shall not bow down to them or worship them; for I, the Lord your God, am a jealous God, punishing the children for the sin of the fathers to the third and fourth generation of those who hate me, but showing love to a thousand generations of those who love me and keep my commandments."

Exodus 20:3–6

"As you go, preach this message: 'The kingdom of heaven is near.'"

Matthew 10:7

Every Christian is either a missionary or an imposter.

CH Spurgeon (1834–1892)

Ram was raised a Hindu. In fact, as an infant he was dedicated to a particular god, and his very devout parents took him to the temple every day all through his childhood. But as a young man he became troubled about many of the things he had been taught, and began to question whether this was really the explanation for life. One day, while he was in a neighbouring town, he encountered Christians for the first time in his life. He only overheard a few sentences, but he couldn't get them out of his mind. Eventually, he tracked down a copy of the Christian Scriptures in a temple library, and started reading it. God's Word gripped him. He read for months, all the way through the Old Testament, and on into the New, until one day he came to the account of the crucifixion of the Lord Jesus. He wept with joy and pain as he asked God to have mercy on him, to forgive him, and as he put his trust in Christ. His family tried to kill him, and he had to escape to another part of India. There, adopted into a Christian home, he became a passionate evangelist. "How badly my people need to learn about Christ!" he says. "I long for them to know that there is one true God, who is utterly good, and utterly loving, and who alone can deliver them from all this deception."

Something old, something new

The trouble with lifting a few verses out of context from the end of one Gospel is that it is conveniently easy to shrug them off. "You've told us how traumatised the disciples were. They were just hallucinating. Or maybe they invented the story to justify starting up a new religion, to trick people into believing their message."

Even within the church, the Great Commission has had its detractors. "I think the Sermon on the Mount is the heart of the Christian message. The Great Commission is alright for those few people whose business it is, but it's not for me." "The Great Commission was for the original disciples, it's not for us today." "Somewhere in the early centuries of the church, the Great Commission got stuck on to the end of the Gospels. It wasn't there originally." (That's almost certainly true in the case of Mark's Gospel. The most reliable early manuscripts we have stop at Mark 16:8.) "It's just an excuse for imperialism."

How do we respond to such charges? It is vital that we do, for even at best they marginalise the Great Commission (especially the bit about reaching the nations: most people are quite keen to retain for themselves inclusion in Christ's statement of authority, and his promise of his presence!). It readily becomes an optional extra relevant solely for the unusually committed, if not the lunatic fringe, among Christians. In particular, "world mission" (at least from a western perspective) becomes something done by a dwindling and embarrassing few "from here" to an increasingly ill-defined "people out there". It has nothing to do with the main life of the church "back here".

In order to deal with these questions, we need first to see whether the Great Commission is an atypical "blip": how far does it represent something radically new, and how far is it simply the restatement of what had been there all along? Is it something tacked on, or is it intrinsic to the whole of God's intention from start to finish, and central to his purposes for his people? Clearly these are extremely crucial issues.

So, we turn from looking directly at the Great Commission as it appears at the end of Matthew's Gospel, and think about the wider biblical witness. How does it fit into Matthew's Gospel as a whole? What clues do we find in the Old Testament, the Bible of our Lord and of the early church till they began to record the New Testament? How did the early church, as recorded in the New Testament, apparently understand it and act upon it?

The Great Commission and Matthew's Gospel

By the time Matthew came to set down his version of the Gospel, of course, he not only knew the whole story he records, he had also had time to reflect on it and on what had happened since in the eventful opening decades of the church's life. That undoubtedly affected the way he wrote. The Gospel is a carefully crafted and deliberately structured book. Its material is selected and organised to highlight certain themes. In particular, Matthew, the most Jewish of the four Gospel writers, emphasises the way in which the Lord Jesus Christ himself, and then both what he said and what he did, fulfils Old Testament prophecy. At the same time, perhaps more than any other Gospel, Matthew also emphasises the place of the Gentiles in the drama that is being played out.

It is possibly for this reason that the early church placed Matthew's Gospel at the very start of the New Testament, as a natural bridge back to the Old Testament, even though by the time the New Testament canon was established the church was more or less entirely Gentile. Matthew legitimises both continuity and newness!

The Gospel begins with a genealogy. Many of us in Western cultures know remarkably little about our ancestors, particularly going back beyond our grandparents. But in many cultures of the world, genealogies are immensely important. They establish your identity. There are several very significant things about the way Matthew records Jesus' ancestry. First, he goes out of his way to mention two non-Jews, Rahab and Ruth, among the list; here are two representatives of "all the nations" drawn into the heart of the people of God. Second, he twice gives Jesus the title "Christ", the Greek form of the Old Testament "Messiah" or "anointed one". This figure is extensively linked, for example by prophets such as Isaiah, with the coming day when all the peoples of the world shall be drawn to worship the God of Israel. Third, he sets Jesus in the line of David, who ruled over the kingdom at the height of its glory, and whose vision for the nations to come to worship God is recorded over and over again in the psalms. And fourth, Jesus' line is traced back to Abraham, the father of the Jewish people, to whom is given the promise that "all peoples on earth will be blessed through you" (Genesis 12:3).

So, tucked into the opening verses of Matthew's Gospel is a wealth of allusion on the one hand to Jesus' Jewishness and on the other to his significance for the whole world. At the other end of the Gospel, as it were balancing the opening genealogy, is the Great Commission. Here, Jesus' identity is defined in terms of his authority over all heaven and earth, and also as the one into whose name, along with the Father and the Spirit, disciples are to be initiated. His significance for the whole world is expressed in terms of "all nations". At the start of the Gospel, the line is traced back through named individuals, one by one; at the end of the Gospel, the inference is that we are looking forward to an unnumbered vast universal community, who are all part of the family of God's people.

In between the opening and the closing of the Gospel, Matthew frequently comes back to the themes of the identity of Jesus Christ and his connection with Old Testament prophecy. At the same time, he repeatedly emphasises the way in which Gentiles as well as Jews are to be included, not excluded, from the blessings God has for humankind. For example, wise men come "from the East" (Matthew 2:1ff) and, with insight that could only have come from God, worship the infant Jesus. Directed by an angel of the Lord, Joseph takes Jesus and Mary to find shelter and safety as refugees in Egypt (Matthew 2:13 ff). A Roman centurion is told that his faith exceeds that of the Jews, and that one day many Gentiles will be found in the kingdom of heaven alongside Abraham, Isaac and Jacob (Matthew 8:5ff). A Canaanite woman's prayer for her demon-possessed daughter is answered (Matthew 15:21 ff).

But also, throughout the Gospel, Matthew unpacks what discipleship means in Jesus' terms, what it means to obey the teaching and to love the Teacher. Task and relationship are interwoven. So, Joseph's love for God and love for Mary enable him to obey the command to care for her and the child that is not his (Matthew 1:18 ff). Obeying the instructions of the Sermon on the Mount is made possible through loving even those who persecute you, in imitation of God's love (Matthew 5:43–48). Pray in quiet confidence, because God is your loving Father (Matthew 7:7–12). Love God extravagantly, with your whole personality, and other people "as yourself", and that will prove the key to all that God has said (Matthew 22:37–40). Take up your cross – symbolically let go of any claim on your life day after day – because genuine discipleship costs everything; and all this for love of Christ whose love for you cost him literal, not symbolic death on a cross (Matthew 16:24). In Matthew chapter 10, the disciples are given an earlier form of the mandate, almost a trial run of what is to come; preaching and demonstrating that "the kingdom of heaven is near" is already shown to be the expected way of life for Jesus' followers. And it is no accident that the command is accompanied by extensive teaching on living with persecution and betrayal, closely followed by an account of John the Baptist's suffering in prison. Discipleship is serious stuff.

By the time Matthew arrives at the Great Commission, the whole of his Gospel illuminates it. And, in turn, the Gospel is clearly set within the context of centuries of Jewish history. No optional add-on. On the contrary, the Great Commission fits hand in glove with all that Jesus has been revealed to be, all that he has taught, all that he has done. And all that Matthew tells us about Jesus fits hand in glove with the sweep of revelation from Genesis onwards. It is to the Old Testament that we must now turn our attention.

The Great Commission and the Old Testament

Far more than many Christians ever grasp, the Old Testament echoes the themes of the Great Commission. While it is sadly true that the Jews frequently misunderstood their calling and their God-intended relationship with other nations, the fact is that over and over again God spells out what is on his heart. This is exactly parallel to the way in which the church has frequently misunderstood her calling and her God-intended relationship with those outside.

The story begins right at the beginning, way back at Creation. From the start, human beings were created in the image of God, and for unclouded friendship with their Creator. This was not God's intention for just some of the human race, or for one particular people group. It was the most fundamental definition of what it is to be a person rather than an animal or any other part of creation. And God's desire for friendship with men and women is, if one may say it reverently, one of the most fundamental things one can say about him. The love that perfectly and mutually flows between the three persons of the Trinity – between Father, Son and Holy Spirit – must also spill over into love for the human beings made by God. It is for this reason that immediately following the catastrophic dis-obedience of Adam and Eve, the Lord comes looking for them. Here is the missionary God in action himself, looking for the lost! To be true to himself, he has to banish sin – and sinners – from his presence. But, also to be true to himself, even in that moment of awful judgement, he compassionately provides for their immediate needs (he clothes them), and hints at the future destruction of sin.

Even the terrible story of Noah and the flood illustrates how God's commitment is to be a Rescuer. It is God himself who comes to Noah and gives him instructions as to how he can be saved from the total destruction that is about to happen. God even entrusts to him the responsibility of preserving representatives of the animal kingdom, so that God's salvation of Noah and his family is mirrored in Noah's role in the saving of the creatures. This is a shadowy paradigm of the Great Commission: salvation is entirely a work of God, and yet the Lord entrusts to men and women a role in the saving of others.

It is with the story of Abraham, however, that God's amazing grace takes on more recognisably the shape that lies behind all that happens subsequently. God first sends Abraham out on a journey. There are no guarantees, no blueprints, other than that as Abraham goes, God will go with him, and that God will know when Abraham has reached his destination. Further, despite Abraham's already considerable age and childlessness, God promises that he is going to make Abraham the father of a very great nation. That in itself would surely be remarkable enough, but there's more. Through Abraham, and through the nation descended from him, all the peoples of the world will be blessed. What did Abraham understand? It's hard to say. But the writer to the Hebrews makes it clear that in obedient faith he did what he was told (Hebrews 11:8). And God kept every one of his promises. He gave Abraham the son through whom in due course came the great nation of Israel. He brought Abraham to the land he had promised, and stayed with him every step of the way. No limited territorial god, this, confined to one small area: here is the God whose authority extends everywhere. Here is the pattern, repeated throughout Scripture, of the meeting point of the particular (one man, one family, one nation, one place) and the universal (all nations, the whole world) precisely because God is God, the one and only true God, God of the entire universe, yet by nature God of personal relationships.

Here, too, is the intriguing balance we noticed in the story of Noah. It is God himself who makes provision to deal with sin, God himself who provides the sacrificial lamb, in the appalling narrative of Abraham preparing to sacrifice his beloved son, Isaac. But from Abraham is required radical discipleship, the willingness to lay down his future in obedience. You can see the tears streaming down his face as he reaches for the knife, you can sense the anguish in his heart. And then, God's dramatic intervention.

It is at this moment that God repeats the promise made when first he called Abraham (Genesis 12:3): "through your offspring all nations on earth will be blessed, because you have obeyed me" (Genesis 22:18). The nation springing from Abraham is not an end in itself. It has a defining purpose. It is to bring blessing – to be a channel of the grace of God – to the nations. It is to be the means by which people "outside" are drawn to know and love and worship the living God, becoming "family".

This is the Great Commission in Old Testament form. Just as the Great Commission of the New Testament is the charter of the church, central to the very purpose of its existence, so the covenant with Abraham is the charter of the people of God throughout the Old Testament. From Genesis 23 to Malachi is the story of how God repeatedly sought to bring his people back to fulfilling the purpose for which they were created, and the story of how God's people obeyed or disobeyed their calling.

Some Old Testament themes

How were the Jewish people to fulfil their purpose? What went right? What went wrong?

In the first place, God's people were the recipients of unique, detailed and progressive revelation from God. Paul tells us in Romans 1:18ff that everybody everywhere has access to limited but crucial truth about God. From the way we ourselves are made as moral beings (the inescapable fact of having been made in the image of God), and from the way the world around us is created, we are faced with the truth: there is an ultimate being who has both eternal power and divine nature to whom we are directly answerable. No person in the world can plead ignorance, though human wickedness suppresses the truth. Even those who have never heard the gospel are accountable to God for how they have responded to this general revelation. But it is to his own people that God revealed himself in great detail. As with everything else, that revelation was entrusted to them not simply for them to live by it but in order that they should pass it on to everyone else so that "the nations could be blessed".

So, the revelation is of the character and nature of God, of the awfulness of sin and the absolute need for salvation, of the ways to relate to God and to the community, of the uniqueness of God and the futility of the gods and idols people made as substitutes. Revelation comes through direct word, through divine action, through inspiration of prophets and teachers, through visual aids such as sacrifices and the Temple, through God's dealings with individuals and with whole communities. Revelation comes in loving grace and terrifying judgement. It comes in narrative and in law, in poetry and in prophecy, in word and in deed.

At every level of this process of revelation, God – the missionary God – is reaching out "to seek and to save". He is telling his people what it is to be lost, and how it is possible to be saved. And, repeatedly, the people of God are being asked to demonstrate to the surrounding nations these great truths – not in order that they may be excluded, but in order that they, too, may respond and be included.

So, there are detailed instructions as to what holy living looks like in concrete terms: behaviour like this, relationships like that. Be what you are! You are made in the image of God, now look increasingly like the original. Then, when other people look on, they'll say, "Ah, this is what God looks like! This is what discipleship looks like!" There are detailed instructions about sin and sacrifice and salvation. So, when other people look on, they'll say, "Ah, this is why God seems far away, or angry! This is how to come close to him and become his family member!"

And there are detailed instructions about how to relate to those of other faiths and other people groups. God's people are not to adapt to the culture of those around them where that culture is in conflict with what God has revealed as compatible with his character. God's people are to be distinctive. If, for example, marriage to someone "outside" means that you will have to conform to his or her religion and culture, you may not do it. But, if he or she will leave behind the old ways and come instead to join you in the worship of the one true and living God, and live according to his ways, then such a marriage is a means of blessing. (In this way, both Rahab of Jericho and Ruth the Moabitess become ancestresses first of great King David, and then of the Lord Jesus.)

In particular, there are on the one hand extensive instructions about hospitality offered to the foreigner or stranger in your midst (along with widows and orphans, they are seen as being especially vulnerable and therefore to be treated with extra special consideration and compassion), and on the other hand unequivocal commands ruthlessly to destroy any hint of worship of idols or other gods that foreigners might bring with them. The people of God must distinguish between people, who are precious, and if possible to be wooed and won to faith, and other faiths, which are based on lies. Isaiah speaks frequently and movingly of the love of God; but he also exposes the sheer folly of idols, which are human creations, and declares the burning anger of God against those who give glory to gods and idols. When it is God's people who divert their worship to other gods, or try to combine worship of God with worship of idols, God's anger knows no bounds; see, for example, the tragic record of Kings and Chronicles. There is absolutely no room for the pluralism so popular in the Western world today.

Always there is this delicate balance between being distinctively different, and winsomely welcoming. Yet this is what it means to be God's people, reflecting his character. For he is surely above all else the one who combines distinctive difference from us with the merciful love which longs to draw us close. The Great Commission, in both Old and New Testaments, is simply an expression of this basic but wonderful truth.

Questions

1. What excuses do Christians commonly give for not obeying the Great Commission? How would you respond to their objections?
2. How could you and your local church more effectively show your neighbourhood what it means to be both distinctively different and winsomely welcoming?
3. Why do you think that God's people in the Old Testament so persistently "tuned out" their missionary calling? What lessons are there for today's church?
4. What do you think the Bible shows us about how God regards other religions and faiths today? As we meet sincere believers of other faiths, how can we demonstrate both God's judgement on all that is so tragically untrue and his compassionate love that would draw people to himself?

3

The King of the Whole Earth

Pentecost transformed the first disciples from fearful, hidden people into bold witnesses to Jesus Christ. The Church was launched into life! But it was also a painful journey to become a community gladly embracing both Jew and Gentile – and new local congregations of young believers needed loving care to nourish them into lively discipleship.

The King of the Whole Earth

Mission is the intentional crossing of barriers from Church to non-church in word and deed for the sake of the proclamation of the Gospel.

Stephen Neill (1900–1984)

Israel's profound problem was not its lack of political freedom but its deep ignorance of God's plan of salvation. The true enemy was not the Roman infidel, but the illusion about God that the people obstinately held to. . . Instead of desiring to be saved from the Gentiles, Israel's mission was to be "a light to the nations, that my salvation may reach to the ends of the earth" (Isaiah 49:6).

Andrew Kirk

There is neither Jew nor Greek, slave nor free, male nor female, for you are all one in Christ Jesus.

Galatians 3:28

To say there is one God and no god but God is not simply an article in a creed. It is an overpowering, brain-hammering, heart-stopping truth that is a command to love the only one worthy of our entire and unswerving allegiance.

Os Guinness

Tears streamed down my face as a young Asian woman threw her arms round me and hugged me. Recently converted out of militant Marxism, and fiercely nationalistic, everything in Anna's background had conditioned her to think of me as her enemy. "I'm so glad you're my sister in the Lord Jesus!" she whispered. "I've never touched a Westerner before! Please be my friend." That Spirit-taught moment of reconciliation between two of

God's children, as different as Jew and Gentile long ago, marked
the beginning of one of the most precious friendships of my life.

How the New Testament church understood the Great Commission

The Jewish people had had some pretty painful experiences at
the hands of other nations over the centuries. War, occupation
of your land by a foreign power, rape of your women, enforced
exile, enslavement, destruction of your homes, your public
buildings and many of the markers of your culture: all these are
deeply traumatic, and Israel and Judah had experienced them
all.

No wonder that by the time of Jesus, the average Jew living
in Palestine, under the uneasy boot of the Roman occupation,
had little love for anyone of another race. By and large,
foreigners spelt trouble, unless of course you could exploit
them, in which case you probably despised them as well. And
no wonder that political and religious aspirations had become so
muddled up. If Messiah was going to be a Deliverer, that had to
mean one who would get rid of the Romans. And that meant
military power and the ability to lead a successful uprising.

On the other hand, the Romans and the Greeks before them
had brought certain advantages, not least a degree of stability
in the region. Of course, you paid for it, in taxes. Large armies,
especially those far from home, are expensive. But, if you
cared to, you could travel long distances without crossing
beyond the borders of the Roman Empire, and that was good
for trade. The Jews liked that. Moreover, mostly you could
travel without fear of bandits, and the Jews liked that, too. And
if, like some four-fifths of the Jews of the day, you had never
come home from some exile or other in the past but settled
down in another country, it was easier than ever to get back to
Jerusalem to look up long-lost relatives, and join in the
festivals of Passover and Pentecost. Every Jew dreamed of

doing that at least once in his lifetime. Even today, as they celebrate Passover, Jews the world over say longingly, "Next year in Jerusalem!" If you'd forgotten your Hebrew, it didn't really matter. The Scriptures had been translated into Greek, the common trade language of the whole Empire, for people in exactly that position, and the synagogues kept your sense of Jewish cultural identity intact.

It was into the buzz and bustle of between-festivals Jerusalem that the disciples returned after that eventful encounter with Jesus on the Galilean mountainside. It was teeming with pilgrim visitors from all over the Empire, and even beyond. No-one with any sense who wasn't a Jew would come to Jerusalem right then – where would you find a hotel bed? – but the place was packed out and every street hummed with a dozen languages. It must have felt electric. The disciples hunkered down to pray and wait for Pentecost.

Whether or not even then they expected what happened next is hard to say. Jesus had promised that the Holy Spirit would come to them as a gift at Pentecost, the festival which celebrated God's provision just as Passover celebrated God's deliverance. The gift is noisy, dramatic and transforming. What is this provision *for*? The answer is absolutely clear. This is not about some private ecstatic experience, it is provision for obeying the Great Commission. For the crowds gather, drawn by the sound of a bunch of down-country Galileans fluently "declaring the wonders of God in our own tongues", and Peter embarks on one of the most extraordinary sermons of all time. He calls on them to repent, be baptised, receive forgiveness and the gift of the Spirit, and to embark on the life of discipleship. As three thousand of them respond, the new-born church has immediately gone international. But it is still Jewish. What happened on this amazing day not only fits with Matthew's version of the Great Commission, but also embraces Luke's special emphasis (Luke 24:47) that "repentance and forgiveness of sins will be preached in his name to all nations, beginning at Jerusalem", and Mark's (Mark 16:17) of signs and wonders. From this day on, the church becomes a community with the Great Commission at its heart, declaring and demonstrating that the kingdom of God is like *this*.

So fervent is the commitment to be and do what the Lord has asked of them, that even the most fearsome persecution does not deter them. On the contrary, the persecution forces the church to disperse from Jerusalem and to scatter in all directions. Which brings them straight back into the loop of the Great Commission: "as you go . . ."! Tourists and pilgrims, traders and homemakers, they are forced from the cosy womb of the intense fellowship of those first few heady months out into their home towns and cities, in an amazing range of countries, to bear witness to all that they had seen and learned.

International though the new church may have been, it seems that the penny has not yet quite dropped. God's concern is not just for Jews, acculturated into many countries but nonetheless still Jews. The apostles are clearly nervous when Philip goes to Samaria (Acts chapter 8) and crowds ask for baptism. But, despite several centuries of estrangement and hostility, at least the Samaritans were half-Jewish by pedigree, and Jesus himself had had a remarkable ministry to a Samaritan woman and her neighbours. Peter and John are sent to check it out, and, seeing evidence of the giving of the Spirit, accept this as an authentic work of God. In Acts chapter 9, another milestone is reached: the Lord stops Saul in his persecuting tracks, to become, so the Lord tells Ananias, "my chosen instrument . . . before the Gentiles" (Acts 9:15). That such a proudly nationalistic Jew should be selected for such a task would have been beyond belief had it not been the Lord himself who was doing the selecting.

And then Acts chapters 10 and 11 record what is undoubtedly the turning point for the apostles. Through an extraordinary vision and God's dealings with Cornelius, Peter is convinced that God wants Gentiles to be received into the believing community. As Luke tells the story, Peter is hardly to be congratulated for winsome tact. Begrudging or shocked, he nonetheless cannot hold out against God:

> You are well aware that it is against our law for a Jew to associate with a Gentile or visit him. But God has shown me that I should not call any man impure or unclean . . . I now realise that God does not show favouritism but accepts men from every nation who fear him and do what is right. (Acts 10:28, 34–5)

When Peter returns to Jerusalem, he has to run the gauntlet of his friends, who accusingly berate him for going into a Gentile home and, worse, actually eating there. Finally, he convinces them that this is truly God's intention, that it was as hard for him to come to terms with as for them, and they reach the momentous conclusion that "God has granted even the Gentiles repentance unto life" (Acts 11:18). It is puzzling for us to grasp just how revolutionary this was for those early Christians, but it is a sobering measure of how far the Jews had abandoned their God-given calling to *bless* the nations. The young church must now absorb the fact that the Great Commission is not given to entrench the blessings of being Jewish, but to recapture their calling to be the channel of God's grace to the whole human race.

From this point on, the historical record of Acts traces exactly that story. On the one hand, Paul and others, going to a place for the first time, would normally seek out the Jewish community first. After all, here there should be those who had a grasp of the Old Testament, who would not first need convincing that there is only one God, the Lord of all, and who should be looking to the coming of the Messiah. On the other hand, whatever the response from the Jews, positive or hostile, the message must also be shared with any Gentile who could be persuaded to listen.

In Chapter 1, we saw how baptising and teaching were both

functions of "making disciples". So it should not surprise us that that is exactly the pattern repeated over and over again in Acts. Sometimes it was possible to stay for a long time and teach the new believers. Sometimes, Paul or Timothy or Barnabas or whoever else, had to move on much sooner. The letters the apostles wrote quickly became part of the discipling process, but there was also considerable movement by Christians for all sorts of reasons. We do not know who all the unnamed "little people" were who quietly moved around and helped young believers become established in their faith, but we do know, for instance from Romans chapter 16, that there must have been many such men and women. As people were initiated into Christ and gathered into believing congregations, they were drawn into discipleship – being taught, being set to serve, and in turn becoming disciple-makers.

The many letters of the New Testament give us a fascinating insight into what was involved in discipling and establishing these early congregations. The letters are written with specific recipients in mind, and therefore address different contexts and needs. But all alike echo the revelation given to God's people in the Old Testament, only now in the light of its fulfilment through the Lord Jesus Christ and the coming of the Holy Spirit. So there is a great deal of teaching about God himself – Father, Son and Holy Spirit – and about what it means to love and trust him. There is teaching about living in a way that mirrors the character of God. There is extensive teaching about dealing with sin and the meaning of salvation. There is teaching about relating to the unbelievers round about, and turning one's back decisively on other religious systems. There is a great deal of teaching about the Lord Jesus Christ as the one and only means of reconciliation with God. And there is teaching about membership of God's family transcending all the barriers of race and social status and gender. What a radical and beautiful message is ours!

Not that we shall experience the kingdom of God in all its

fullness until we get to heaven; but, at the same time and paradoxically, the kingdom has already been ushered in with Christ. So, we are here and now to live our lives as subjects of that King, unseen just now but soon to return. When he returns, it will be simultaneously as gladly awaited Saviour and as awesome Judge. In the meantime, whenever people are healed or delivered from demons, whenever there is victory over sin in a person's life, whenever a community that would naturally be enemies are able to live together in harmony because of the transforming grace of God, there the kingdom has broken into the here and now, giving us and the watching world a little glimpse of what it means to be under the rule of the King.

The Old Testament, especially latterly, points with longing to the coming Messiah who will establish the kingdom. The New Testament says that in Christ the Messiah has already come, and we have seen the kingdom. But, we too look forward with longing to the Messiah's coming, this time his coming again. In the meantime, the church is to be the highway along which the blessing of God flows out in all directions to all the peoples of the world.

Questions

1. Why do you think many early Jewish Christians found it so difficult to accept the truth that God loved Gentiles (non-Jews) as well? What parallels are there in the Church today?

2. In what ways is God's love for the whole world – not just parts of it – rooted in his character?

3. What examples can you think of in your own life where you have been very slow to understand what God has clearly said? How might we help one another to grow in understanding and in obedience?

4. How could your local church or fellowship become more multicultural?

4

Living as the People of God

How does our calling as the people of God work out in practice? How will we live, and what will motivate us, so that we are in fact the missionary people we are called to be? In this chapter, we look at a few of the characteristics of life as disciples.

Living as the People of God

After this I looked and there before me was a great multitude that no-one could count, from every nation, tribe, people and language, standing before the throne and in front of the Lamb . . . And they cried out in a loud voice: "Salvation belongs to our God, who sits on the throne, and to the Lamb."

Revelation 7:9–10

I place no value on anything I have or may possess, except in relation to the kingdom of Christ. If anything will advance the interests of the kingdom, it shall be given away or kept, only as by giving or keeping it I shall most promote the glory of him to whom I owe all my hopes in time and eternity.

David Livingstone (1813–1873)

How is it possible that the gospel should be credible, that people should come to believe that the power which has the last word in human affairs is represented by a man hanging on a cross? I am suggesting that the only answer, the only hermeneutic of the gospel, is a congregation of men and women who believe it and live by it.

Lesslie Newbigin (1909–1998)

"What was it", I asked him, "that made you want to become a disciple of Jesus Christ? Surely you knew it would bring you all sorts of trouble?" Without a moment's hesitation, the young man replied, "It was first of all the love of a Christian family for me, and for one another, that grabbed my attention. Then, when their son was killed in a car accident, I was stunned that despite their very real grief they could forgive the person responsible, they weren't angry with God – they said they could trust him because he loved them and they loved him – and they were quite sure that James was in heaven. That was the beginning. The way they lived, and lived up to what they said, made me want to discover more about the Lord." Soon after, he returned to his home country. He wrote and told me that when – not if – I heard that he had died, to remember that he would rather die a Christian than live a Muslim, and that he regretted nothing. That was the last time I heard from him. But a while later, by a roundabout route, I was told that his family had poisoned him when he wouldn't deny Christ.

Living as the people of God

We have already seen that, embraced by the Lord's authority and the promise of his presence, the core calling of God's people, as expressed in the Great Commission, is to make disciples. Put at its simplest, that means that our lives are to be focused on God – the God and Father of our Lord Jesus Christ – and on enabling others also to focus their lives on him. But, to unpack the scope of the Great Commission a little more, we need to explore further what the life of discipleship entails.

Living in the name of the Trinity

In the Bible, "name" and character or person are very closely interwoven. The names of men and women are often very significant, and frequently they explain what the bearer will do or become one day in the future. So, the angel tells Joseph that Mary's baby is to be named Jesus, which is the Greek form of Joshua ("the Lord saves") "because he will save his people from their sins" (Matthew 1:21). And Matthew adds the comment that Jesus is the fulfilment of the prophecy of Isaiah 7:14: ". . . they will call him Immanuel", which means, "God with us".

In the Great Commission, baptism is to be "in the name of the Father and of the Son and of the Holy Spirit" (Matthew 28:19). This is clearly very specific, and understood very explicitly by the emerging church. For example, when Paul went to Ephesus (Acts chapter 19), he discovered disciples who had received John's baptism (for repentance) but had not yet been baptised into the name of Jesus nor received (or even heard of) the Holy Spirit. Paul's immediate response is to baptise them again, this time into identification with Jesus, and the Spirit comes to them. Almost certainly, this parallels what happened at Pentecost. Probably there were among the crowds some, if not many, who had been baptised by John. But Peter urges them to "Repent and be baptised, every one of you, in the name of Jesus Christ for the forgiveness of your sins. And you will receive the gift of the Holy Spirit" (Acts 2:38). It really matters, it seems, that baptism and initiation is "into" the right name.

So what is this all about? It is precisely that "the name" is not simply a collection of symbols in sound or writing, but the very being and person to whom it points.

We are to be baptised, and baptise, into the name of God the Father because this name, from a New Testament perspective, embraces most clearly the revelation of God in the Old Testament, and takes on new glories in the New. All that Jahweh, the Lord, is in the Old Testament, is encompassed here. The name "Father" reminds us that here is the one from whose creative will we (and indeed the whole universe) have sprung. It reminds us of the unity of the human race. It reminds us that this is no mere tribal god but the one and only true and living God, the Ultimate, beyond and beside whom there is no-one else, the Father whom everyone everywhere needs to know. It reminds us that the Lord Jesus ("This is my Son, whom I love; with him I am well pleased", attested by the Father at Jesus' baptism and transfiguration), in his earthly ministry, had complete divine authorization. It reminds us that God created us to live in loving relationship with himself. God is not some far distant, aloof and unknowable being. He is our Father.

We are to be baptised, and baptise, into the name of the Son because he is the Lord Jesus Christ. "Lord" reminds us of his kingly authority on earth and in heaven: there is nowhere outside his jurisdiction. He is the Boss, and nobody, anywhere at all, can evade that. He is the one who will come again one day in glory but also in devastating judgement. He is the one who has absolute rights over our lives, and discipleship is simply a recognition of that. "Jesus" reminds us that we are sinners in need of being rescued, and that here is the one who through his life and death and resurrection makes salvation possible. Indeed, as Peter declared in an early sermon, "Salvation is found in no-one else, for there is no other name under heaven given to men by which we must be saved" (Acts 4:12). It reminds us, too, because this is his earthly name, that in Jesus God became fully human. "Christ" reminds us that the Lord Jesus was the fulfilment of God's open promise from many centuries in advance, that he was the deliberately chosen one to deal with the cosmic fall-out from human disobedience in Genesis chapter 3.

And lastly, we are to be baptised, and to baptise, into the name of the Holy Spirit because here is God in all his life-giving, present, transforming power. Here is God in the here-and-now, equipping God's people to be what they are supposed to be, and to do what they are supposed to do. Here is God taking the words and lives of ordinary everyday Christians and using them to "convict the world of guilt in regard to sin and righteousness and judgment" (John 16:8). Here is "the Spirit of truth who goes out from the Father" and testifies to the Son (John 15:26).

So, we are to be baptised, and to baptise, into this very specific person who is God. The Trinitarian formula very deliberately spells out for us exactly who he is and makes it totally clear to whom we are to give our life-long allegiance, expressed in discipleship. All that the whole Bible has to say about God is gathered up. We cannot select parts and reject others. Properly understood, the Great Commission is inseparable from the whole of Scripture, and from all that God is and ever has been. It is this God, and no other, whose name is "high over all".

Living in community

Discipleship was never intended to be a solo pursuit. On the contrary, because there is community within the Godhead, human beings also are designed for relationship with others. It is in community that we experience and express love, forgiveness, compassion, justice, nurture, growth, and a host of other good things. Of course, it is sadly equally true that it is in community we can experience and express the reverse of all these, where God's blueprint for social relationships is ignored, or where God's resources through the Holy Spirit are not drawn upon. But, nonetheless, it is God's intention that in families, "tribes" (and their equivalents), and other social groupings, we should interact with one another in such a way as to enable people to keep learning and developing. In particular, it is within the community of the worshipping congregation, that is, the community of committed believing people, that Christian discipleship should flourish.

This is one of the reasons why Christian mission must always have as a goal the establishing of properly functioning Christian communities: local churches that live out the truth about God. This is much more complex than simply being in church together on Sunday mornings! Ever since the Fall, people have naturally been at odds with each other, seeking to dominate and manipulate, to exploit, each one to his or her own advantage. By contrast, the Lord Jesus said, "By this all men will know that you are my disciples, if you love one another" (John 13:35). Keeping God's commandments (rather than just talking about them) and loving our fellow human beings is strong evidence of true love for God. This is clearly not some vague emotion, but rather the costly practical daily lifestyle that puts the glory of God and the wellbeing of others above self-interest. It is the pattern of lives deeply interwoven, not just occasionally and briefly brushing against each other. So telling is such a way of life demonstrated in a community, and so powerful the unity it shows, that outside observers will say, "Wow, Jesus must be who he claimed to be to produce that effect!" (John 17:23). This is no easy calling. That is why on the one hand much of the Scriptures is devoted to telling us how to live like this, and on the other hand why the Holy Spirit's superhuman transforming power is so essential.

Living in community, then, is both the means of individual Christians making progress in their own life as disciples, and the relationship by which groups of Christians together grow in ways impossible otherwise. It is also the visual aid which demonstrates the truth and power of God to the outsider. In those places in today's world where any kind of overt Christian community is prevented by the State, discipleship is a very lonely and difficult business. In his mercy, God can deal with the most isolated believer and pour grace into his life. But, it is not the way it was intended to be. The intention was that God's people should minister to one another, encouraging one another to press on to know and love God more deeply, and bringing a variety of gifts and temperaments together to enrich one another. Such living is especially a challenge to Western Christians. Many of us come from cultures that today are both strongly individualistic and also very selfish. In such a setting, true Christian discipleship is intensely counter-cultural. Living in community, as the evidence of true discipleship, will model justice and mercy, compassion and forgiveness, love and joy, grace and generosity. None of these Christian fundamentals is possible without relationships.

Living as priests

The priest of the Old Testament had an awesome responsibility. He stood between God and men and women. He represented his people to God, seeking mercy on their behalf. He represented God to the people, explaining what God required of them. And, standing between God and the people, he performed the sacrifices. These were a symbolic acting out of the need for sin to be dealt with, and human dependence upon the grace and mercy of God if there was to be escape from destruction, children to be born and reared safely, or even food on the table. For God held all the power of life and death in his hands, and in performing the sacrifices the priest was acknowledging that.

The Lord Jesus Christ is described paradoxically as both sacrifice ("the Lamb of God who takes away the sin of the world" John 1:29) and priest ("when this priest – Jesus Christ – had offered for all time one sacrifice for sins, he sat down at the right hand of God" Hebrews 10:12). He supremely represents God to man and man to God. He alone, fully God and fully man, could stand entirely in the place of both God and human beings. Even in heaven and eternity, he is seen as both sacrifice and King, "the Lamb upon the throne".

The language of sacrifice, especially of blood sacrifice, is very alien to modern Westerners, although in some cultures it is still a familiar part of everyday life. But in the Scriptures the language of sacrifice and priesthood is inescapable and pervasive. In the Old Testament, the great event of the Passover towers over subsequent history. In every home in Egypt, Egyptian and Israelite alike, there was a death: either a firstborn son, or a firstborn lamb. Those who chose to take God seriously discovered that the blood of the lamb, painted clearly on the door, was accepted in the place of the death of a son. The lamb bore the impact of judgement. In the New Testament, the old sacrificial system, only ever a picture of a far deeper reality, is swept away as the Lord Jesus dies bearing the impact of judgement on sin. This is what it takes for God to make peace with humankind. It is this which opens up the way for God to accomplish what he is, the missionary God who seeks and saves his beloved creation. So, at Jesus' birth, the shepherds can abandon their sheep – the sheep on the hillsides outside Bethlehem, jealously guarded to be perfect for sacrifices in the Temple – because the Saviour who renders all other sacrifice superfluous has come into the world.

Against such a background it is surely amazing that Peter should write these words to a group of young churches: "You are . . . a royal priesthood . . . a people belonging to God, that you may declare the praises of him who called you out of darkness into his wonderful light" (1 Peter 2:9). God's people are called to represent God to man and man to God: to declare and live out what God has done, and to pray for those who need to be brought to God. We bring, as it were, the sacrifice of Jesus before the world: "This is what he has done for you, and why!" We bring, as it were, the sacrifice of Jesus before the Father: "This is what your Son has done. Have mercy, Lord!" Discipleship is priesthood: not a formal office, but a way of life, with the saving death of the Lord Jesus at its heart. Think about it. Once only *a chosen few* acted out the drama of sacrifice and priesthood; and they did only act it out. Now, following the decisive sacrifice and priesthood of Christ *the Chosen One*, the whole of God's people – *the chosen many* – carry the message of sin forgiven and of the eternal perfect priest who "always lives to intercede" (Hebrews 7:25).

Living in the light of Christ's return

While the Old Testament points to the first coming of Christ, and the New Testament describes it and reflects on it, much of the New Testament also points to his second coming. Repeatedly, God's people are urged to live fully in the here-

and-now, yes, but at the same time on tiptoe in expectant faith looking for the Lord's return. This will change the way we live, our values and priorities. And it will change the way we think about the Great Commission.

Down through the centuries of the church, there have always been people who have held extreme views and engaged in extreme actions in relation to the Second Coming of Christ. At frequent intervals, someone or another has declared that Christ will return on such and such a date. Usually they have whipped up intense speculation and often persuaded many followers to do bizarre things, even to the point, tragically, in some cases of committing mass suicide.

Where the church today lives in the context of great poverty or of low life expectancy, Christians often have a much more consistent and faith-full expectation that the Lord is coming back. In the very best, and biblical, sense, it is a source of great hope. But, in many wealthier countries, where life expectancy is high and where materialism can readily seduce even Christian men and women without their really noticing it, the fact of the Lord's return is one of those things you pay lip service to but it doesn't actually make much difference to everyday life. Security is (mis)placed in possessions and healthcare. The odd things that have happened in the past add to the discrediting of what is in fact a very central part of biblical teaching. Further, in the West, our cultures are very impatient: we want everything, even in religion, right now. Sadly, some Christians have been misled by this into wanting all the pleasures of heaven here and now on earth, and have tailored their thoughts about discipleship accordingly.

But, Christ's disciples are called on to live "in the light of his coming". Why does it matter so much? The Bible tells us that it should greatly motivate us to take discipleship and godly living very seriously. We are accountable to God, and when Christ returns it will be as reigning King and awesome Judge. For those who have turned their back on God, there will be no escape from terrible destruction. For love of God (who longs for everyone everywhere to come to the knowledge of God and to turn to him in repentance and trust) and in compassion for humanity, Christians should be spurred on by the reality of the Second Coming to urgent and patient evangelism. Moreover, we are to share not only the reality and inescapability of judgement, we are also to share the joyful prospect of heaven for those who trust in Christ.

To be sure, there are many things that are puzzling, especially in the books of Daniel and of Revelation, and it is sad when Christians fall out with each other over details of timetable and suchlike. But alongside the things that are hard to understand there are plenty of truths which shine out. Among them is the clear teaching that heaven is a glorious place to be, where we shall be joyfully taken up with loving God perfectly, where we shall see the Lord in all his glory, and be surrounded by perfection in every way. Further, there is the repeated promise that there will be representatives from every tribe and tongue and nation joined together in worship around the throne of God. Here, the Great Commission finds its marvellous fulfilment.

Did the first disciples believe Christ would return within their lifetime? It is difficult to know, but there are certainly hints to that effect, and it seems that it spurred them on to passionate service, even when that put their lives at risk. The biblical emphasis is that since we do not know when Christ will return, we are to live in readiness for him to come at any moment.

In one of the passages of Jesus' teaching about the end of time as we know it, and in the context of teaching about terrible suffering on the one hand and about false teachers on the other, there comes this intriguing statement: "And this gospel of the kingdom will be preached in the whole world as a testimony to all nations, and then the end will come" (Matthew 24:14). Later, Peter wrote this: "You ought to live holy and godly lives as you look forward to the day of God and speed its coming" (2 Peter 3:11–12). Christians have puzzled over the meaning of these verses. Are they to be understood very literally, in which case some believe that by "planning" world mission country by country they can ensure the Lord returns sooner than otherwise he might? Or are they to be understood as Hebrew idioms which simply tell us that the gospel and the church are universal, and that "the end" will surely come (but without any causal connection); and that "speeding Christ's coming" means "wait eagerly for it" (as many translators believe)? Perhaps we shall not know for sure till we get to heaven. In the meantime, the need both to live holy lives and to preach the gospel to all nations are clearly attested elsewhere, and for these we should have no reservations.

Living in the world

Authentic discipleship must be lived out in the real world. It is not about living in a ghetto, or in a moated castle with the drawbridge raised! God created men and women to look after the earth and all that is in it – its resources, the animal and plant kingdoms, as well as the whole human race. So, discipleship must model responsible work and attention to ecological health as well as (or even as part of) reconciliation with God and with one another. Both Old and New Testaments have a great deal to say about these responsibilities, and if we are to be faithful disciples and disciple-makers we must take them seriously, too.

Sadly, in the past couple of centuries, Westerners in particular have had the means of exploiting the earth's natural resources, and of engaging in very intensive agricultural policies, so that much harm has been done. In very recent years, ecological awareness has become a fashionable cause, sometimes as enlightened self-interest ("We are suffering as a result of these abuses of nature", "We want our children to grow up in a world that still has tigers"), and sometimes out of a genuine sense that we are accountable stewards of something that does not ultimately belong to us. There is growing recognition that there are tragic consequences when we ignore the delicate balance God has designed between different parts of the natural world. If we denude a mountain of its trees without phased replanting, we should not be surprised if soon there are devastating floods. If we hunt a species of predator to extinction, we should not be surprised if its natural prey becomes too populous. Every part of God's creation has a unique and vital function.

This does not, of course, mean that we should never seek to control or bring about careful change. We are, after all, called to work in, and take care of, God's world (Genesis 2:15), and to rule over it and subdue it (Genesis 1:28). Further, the impact of the Fall was truly cosmic, affecting not just human beings but the whole of creation. Just as God wants to root out the sin and its consequences in our lives, so we should seek to counteract the consequences of the Fall in the natural world. We rightly try to remove the choking thistles out of the crops, or seek effective treatment for disease rather than fatalistically leave millions to die too soon. But, we will do these things with a humble heart, and acknowledge that we are accountable tenants in God's world, not autonomous masters of it.

On the other hand, we will not fall into the trap of elevating the animal kingdom to equality with human beings. Men and women are not simply "another species" of animal. At Creation, only men and women were made in God's image. It is only human beings who can enter into full companionship with God. The Lord Jesus came in human, not animal, form. Adam and Eve were instructed to serve as God's representatives in ruling over the natural world, not the other way about. People have a unique place in God's creation.

What has this got to do with being Great Commission Christians? Simply that our lives of discipleship must be lived out in the real context of the real world. Wise and responsible relationship to that world around us is a vital visual aid declaring that we recognise the living God as its personal Creator, that we know the reality of both fallenness and grace, and that we care about those with whom we share the earth. It points to God's promise that one day, when the Lord returns, there will be a new heaven and a new earth, where everything is in perfect harmony. It tells a watching world something crucial about our faith.

Living with suffering and martyrdom

Jesus' call to his disciples to follow him was not a call to immediate and life-long enjoyment and partying (though one glorious day we shall feast in heaven at the greatest party of all eternity!). "Take up your cross!" he said.

Of course we prefer a comfortable life. That is only natural. Nonetheless, if we are to be like our Master, suffering is inescapable. As light shows up the darkness, a godly life will always sooner or later arouse resentment in those who are shamed, or sense themselves to be judged, by it.

The invitation of the gospel is truly an invitation of grace; but it not an invitation to ease – except that deep-down ease of a conscience at peace with God. It is an invitation to a life-long commitment to making choices, day in, day out, to be single-minded: to follow Christ, wherever he leads, whatever the circumstances, whatever the cost. For him, it meant the relinquishing of all the glory and splendour of heaven to come to the dirt and poverty of peasant life in first century Palestine. It meant leaving the worship and recognition which was eternally his by right to come to people who did not know who he was and who finally condemned him to the cruellest of deaths. "God, contracted to a span" says the hymn: God shrunken to the size of a man's hand. We don't care to be shrunk: we fear being diminished. Yet, for Jesus, *and for us*, this is the pathway to fulfilment beyond all human imagination.

Paul once put it like this: "I want to know Christ and the power of his resurrection and the fellowship of sharing in his sufferings, becoming like him in his death, and so, somehow, to attain to the resurrection from the dead" (Philippians 3:10–11). The fact is, you can't have resurrection until first you have suffered and died. Identification with the one presupposes identification with the other. We do not have to be masochists, seeking suffering and pain for its own sake. If we walk the way of authentic discipleship, though, it will be costly as well as glorious.

In some parts of the world, Christians suffer greatly at the hands of hostile forces in their particular communities. Almost from the very beginning of the church, there have been those called to give their lives as martyrs. For most of us, that will not be the case. But, whoever we are, being disciples, and being disciple-makers, is a call to share in Christ's sufferings, and to put our lives on the line. We do that secure in the knowledge that "all authority" does not lie in the hands of those who make us suffer, but in the hands of our Lord. And those hands bear the marks of crucifixion, the guarantee of his love. Further, whatever the suffering, he does not abandon us in it, for he has given his word to be with us "to the end of the age".

Questions

1. Using the themes suggested in this chapter, pause and think about each in turn. How far is your life as a disciple, and that of your church, an effective illustration of each one?

2. What practical lifestyle changes do you think you may need to make in order to live more clearly as "the people of God"?

3. What do you think is the inter-relationship between the themes suggested in this chapter and growing in love for God?

4. In particular, in cultures obsessed with the present and the immediate and the visible, how can we live more profoundly "in the light of his coming again" and the reality of heaven?

PART II

Vignettes from History

In the first part of this book, we have seen that the Great Commission is not some optional postscript, but rather that it is part and parcel of the whole revelation of God's purposes for his people in time preparing for eternity. Throughout the Bible we find the same theme: God wants to have people the world over drawn into reconciled relationship with himself, and his people are the means by which that message is to be communicated. We have also seen that the Great Commission is both wide and deep in scope, wide because God's heart yearns over everybody everywhere in every generation, and deep because discipleship and the making of disciples can never be fully completed this side of heaven.

Perhaps it may seem that we have ranged over Scripture more widely than is customary when thinking about the Great Commission. This is precisely because wherever we turn, from Genesis to Revelation, the witness of Scripture is the same. God is a missionary God, and the people of God are to be a missionary people. In the Western church today, we badly need to recapture this fundamental truth.

In Part Two, we turn our attention to how the church has responded to its missionary calling down through the centuries.

5

Getting Started

Why did God choose just the moment he did to send his Son into the world? And why did God allow his church to begin in such weakness and vulnerability, and often through persecution? In this chapter we begin to trace the story of the church, from Pentecost till the end of the first century.

Getting Started

While they were stoning him, Stephen prayed, "Lord Jesus, receive my spirit." Then he fell on his knees and cried out, "Lord do not hold this sin against them." When he had said this, he fell asleep. And Saul was there, giving approval to his death.

Acts 7:59–8:1

There is nothing of which it is more difficult to convince men than that the providence of God governs this world.

John Calvin (1509–1564)

For eighty and six years I have been his [Christ's] servant, and he has done me no wrong, and how can I blaspheme my King who saved me?

Polycarp the Martyr (AD 69–155)

Besides being put to death they [the Christians] were made [by Nero] to serve as objects of amusement; they were clad in the hides of beasts and torn to death by dogs; others were crucified, others set on fire to serve to illuminate the night when daylight failed.

Tacitus (1st century historian)

It would be hard to imagine anyone much more marginalised than Mrs Bong. In a poor community, she was one of the very poorest of the poor, living in the flimsiest of shacks made of old boxes and a sheet of polythene. At twenty-five, abandoned by her man, and having already borne seven children, all but one of whom had died in infancy, she looked as if she were fifty. And then she contracted leprosy. Hounded out of her neighbourhood, she fled to the only refuge she knew of – a tiny clinic run by two missionary nurses. Through their compassion and long-term care, Mrs Bong was not only eventually healed physically but also became a disciple of the Lord Jesus Christ. She went back to the very poor who were "her people", and, living again among them, and sharing the precariousness of such extreme poverty, became the catalyst for a little congregation of worshippers. "How else," she asked, "could I have shared God's love with them in a way they could understand?"

"I will build my church!"

It would be a happy thing to be able to say that from Pentecost onwards the church has always been committed to mission, with full understanding, and in a biblical manner. Unfortunately, that would not be true.

Yet, it wouldn't be true either to say that the church has rarely been involved in mission. The fact is that wherever the church has been in all its history, the manner in which it has (or has not) incorporated people into its own ranks, and the way in which it has related to those outside its ranks, has demonstrated its convictions about mission. The message it has proclaimed and the life it has lived out, the measure in which it has incarnated Christ in word and deed, and the extent to which it has conformed to the kingdom of God – all these have recorded, intentionally or by default, the tale of how mission and the Great Commission have been understood. The convictions may have been skewed or defective, or on the other hand getting close to biblical norms, but inescapably they have always shown *something*. The ways in which Christians live and relate and teach in any given context display (and sometimes betray!) their essential presuppositions about being disciples of Jesus Christ.

In this section, we shall explore some of the variety of models by which the church has related to the world beyond its own community, and through which it has sought to disciple those within. Of course, the whole story is known only to God himself. Certainly, and sadly, many Christians have dismissed as irrelevant or "not truly Christian" what has happened in traditions other than their own, leaving their understanding of church history greatly impoverished. So, for example, for centuries Orthodox and Roman Catholic and Protestant streams of the church largely ignored or despised one another, and occasionally fought each other bitterly, with words or weapons or both. Even within those streams, especially the Protestant stream, there has often been woeful ignorance or hostility between one tributary and another.

While the differences between these various parts of the church are often profound, and the doctrinal issues dividing them are serious, nonetheless it is important for us to try to stand back and see what God has been doing on the widest possible canvas. The truth of the matter is that no tradition does everything right, and no tradition does everything wrong. We may not simplistically say that anything outside our own tradition is not the life of the church at all. Perhaps if we had more humility we might have wider vision, and greater cause to praise God. It is sad that much of the story has been largely inaccessible across the traditions, because of barriers of language and prejudice. To this day, church history books do not adequately reflect the worldwide story.

Quite apart from the complex interplay between grace and fallenness in God's people, a great tangle of convictions, personalities, circumstances and cultures has contributed to the very diverse ways in which the church has operated in different places and at different times. Even within the pages of the New Testament, we find evidence of different ways of engaging with the good news about Jesus. This can be seen starkly in the tension within the Jewish Christian community as they came to terms with the emergence of the Gentile Christian community. It can also be seen in the different ways in which Paul writes to various young churches, each learning to live as a believing family in a unique cultural context. Paul never stopped being deeply rooted in his Jewish identity, but he fought passionately for the freedom for believers, led by the Holy Spirit and within the boundaries of truth, to be disciples of Jesus Christ, not disciples of Judaism. In a variety of forms, this issue has haunted the church all down through the centuries, as one group or another has sought to establish conformity to its own traditions rather than first and foremost to Jesus Christ.

Some of the tension in the very early years arose out of prejudice or out of failure to grasp the momentous nature of what God was doing. Some of it arose out of the genuine difficulty of discerning the difference between the essential gospel and the variety of cultural clothing in which it might legitimately appear. Some of it, especially later, arose out of growth. As the church spread, numerically and geographically and culturally, how could it keep the different parts in step with each other? It was fatally simple to rely on structures and organisation and man-made regulations. And so, too often, as the church became institutionalised, this pattern was repeated: organic, Spirit-led life gave way to something much more artificial and external, people jockeyed for power and control rather than following in the footsteps of the Suffering Servant, and valid diversity was manhandled into uniformity.

Despite all that, the story of the spread of the church should make us shout for joy, and adore the God who made it all happen. Two thousand years after that little band of men trudged the dusty roads back to Jerusalem to wait for the coming of the Holy Spirit, the church is truly worldwide. Yes, there are great swathes of humankind who have no access at present to the good news about Jesus, and we should find that shocking, spurring us to repentance and determination to see that dramatically changed. But, at the same time there is a very real sense in which Christianity is today a world faith, with followers of Jesus all over the globe.

How did this happen? Here we can only look at a few tiny snapshots from down the intervening years, between Pentecost and today. This is only a fraction of the story, but over and over again it is abundantly clear that it is less our story and more God's story. Repeatedly, it becomes clear that even the best efforts of Christian men and women have been flawed. "But God!" Here is "amazing grace": through the best and the worst, and everything in between, God has not been thwarted from keeping his promise. He has been, he is, he will be, building his church until in his sovereign will it is brought to completion, and time gives way to eternity.

Preparing the scene

"When the time had fully come," writes Paul, "God sent his Son . . ." (Galatians 4:4). We could translate that, "when the moment was just right!" There is a lovely sense of divine preparation and sovereign organisation of affairs so that everything was in place for the momentous event of the birth and life, the death and resurrection, of God's Son – and thus of the church.

This is marvellous faith-nurturing stuff! We could be so taken up with all the apparent weaknesses of the scenario that we be tempted to think God made some bad strategic mistakes. After all, wasn't Palestine just a two-bit obscure country, powerless under a pagan imperial ruler? Wasn't Jesus Christ a vulnerable baby conceived in odd circumstances by an unmarried teenage mother, then a refugee, then a poor artisan, then a wandering preacher who couldn't travel faster than the plod of a donkey or further than a few dozen miles from home? Didn't he die as a criminal, abandoned by almost everybody? Weren't the early disciples an incompetent bunch of unskilled and uneducated misfits?

So how come that Paul could say so confidently that the God who could have chosen any place, and any point in history, made this exactly the right time and place? If we had been the organising committee, we wouldn't have done things like this!

Yet, even a little historical study shows us how remarkable a moment this was, and how marvellously God had "organised" an amazing combination of circumstances. The very political and historical and religious factors that we might have deemed disastrous became the launching pad of the fledgling church.

It would have been a rare Jew who loved the Romans. Who likes to be a subject nation? Yet, even the most nationalistic Jew knew that the Romans had brought peace and stability around the Mediterranean world after centuries of war and political precariousness. He knew that for the moment they did not live under the shadow of unpredictable and imminent invasion, where alien armies would march back and forth through his little country, carrying off another wave of captives while they were at it. He knew that the Romans had brought stable law and order, built an amazing network of good roads, and made travel both on those roads and on the traffic lanes of the seas largely safe from banditry and piracy. He knew that with no frontiers he could move easily over many hundred miles, through surrounding countries, and engage freely in trade in any of them. Further, however galling it might be to have Roman soldiers garrisoned in every major town or city, he knew that by and large the Jews enjoyed a very privileged status: they were not, like many of their neighbours, enslaved; and they had the right to follow their Jewish faith without interference. They could meet freely in their synagogues, worship and sacrifice in the Temple, retain the Sanhedrin with significant powers, and be exempt from the various pagan practices required from most Gentiles. In some respects, having to pay tax to the Romans was a small price compared with what might have been.

Thanks to the Greeks, who briefly but brilliantly preceded the Romans as the imperial power throughout the region, there was even a common language. Perhaps for the first time since Babel, people of many different ethnic backgrounds and from a wide geographical area could communicate freely. To be sure, the free communication of the Judeo-Christian message was hardly the agenda of either the Greeks or of the Romans, but it was clearly God's. Because of waves of exile, perhaps as many as four-fifths of all Jews lived outside Palestine. Those who had been away from "home" for several generations had often lost their familiarity with Hebrew, and, anxious to conserve the Jewish faith among them, scholars had translated the Old Testament into the Greek version known as the Septuagint. This meant that the majority of Jews were familiar with using Greek language and categories for expressing their monotheistic faith, and the story of their people. So when the early church came to write down the New Testament, the rich Greek language was a readily accessible vehicle – and Gentiles coming to faith could immediately have access to the Old Testament as well as the New. Indeed, because of the use of Greek, already by the time of Christ many men and women from the Gentile communities had been attracted by many aspects of Jewish belief and teaching, and had become proselytes or "God-fearers", that is, those who turned their backs on paganism and embraced monotheism. Some of these were among the first of the Gentiles to become Christians.

Further, the periods of exile and dispersion, and the times of separation from or destruction of the Temple in Jerusalem, had given rise to the synagogues as places where the Jewish faith could be kept alive and transmitted within the community. For many Jews, this gave a much stronger sense of living out their faith where they were, rather than being highly dependent on what took place in the Temple itself. You might long to make the journey to Jerusalem at least once in a lifetime, to celebrate Passover and Pentecost, but for most Jews for most of their lives synagogue and home must be the focal points for religious life. This shift also helped them make the transition to relying on the teacher rather than the priest, at least in everyday and practical terms. When the church was born, this detachment from the Temple and any one geographical location, and the recognised role of the teacher, were to be crucially important.

We already see here some exciting principles to help us think more clearly about the Great Commission. Firstly, we should be looking eagerly to see what it is in any given context that God is doing that can become a springboard for the gospel. We should be looking in faith and expectation, because, however unlikely the circumstances, God is committed to keep his promise to build his church. Secondly, what matters is not political freedom or social or economic power. On the contrary, there may be great weakness in all these areas. What does matter is discerning what God is doing, making his word – oral and written – available in language understood by the people, engaging in imaginative movement around the world, reaching out to communities where they are.

So God had set the scene. What happened next?

Out of weakness

On various occasions, for example in John 17:18 and John 20:21, the Lord Jesus states that he sends his disciples into the world in the same way in which the Father sent him. What way was that? Surely, the pattern of the Gospels and of the Epistles after them consistently underscores that it was in weakness and vulnerability, in pouring himself out in self-sacrifice. The magnificent early church hymn, quoted by Paul in Philippians 2:6–11, expresses this in a breathtaking manner. Here is the One whose home was the perfection and glory of heaven, who for our sakes voluntarily relinquished wealth and status and absolute power. At every point of his life and death, from birth in a borrowed stable, to burial in a borrowed tomb, this principle of weakness is inescapable. Well, says Jesus, this is the way in which I send those who follow me, too.

It is important to grasp this, because it helps us to understand why in the wisdom of God the Christian movement did not begin in the imperial palace in Rome, and why the truest growth of the church has often come in the context of powerlessness and persecution, of suffering and marginalisation, of hatred and poverty. Indeed, it seems that whenever the church has abandoned these principles and pressed forward through power and wealth, or by force and violence, there may have been temporary apparent gains but these have soon given way to the gravest of problems and the compromising of the gospel.

In the wake of Pentecost, the early church had no earthly power, only the power of the Holy Spirit and of love and faith and truth. They had neither significant wealth nor property, no political or ecclesiastical clout. Within days, the bitter opposition that had been directed towards the Lord Jesus came to be focused on the disciples instead. But, they persisted in explaining what God had done and was doing, they urged repentance and a new way of life on all who would listen, and they developed an extraordinarily powerful pattern of loving community life. All of this was wrapped up in a sensitivity to the activity of the Holy Spirit among them, constantly refreshed through prayer and worship. It was borne out not only by the turning to faith of many, but also by the continuation of the miracles of healing and deliverance previously displayed through the Lord Jesus.

Persecution soon scattered believers in all directions, loosening the dependency on Jerusalem. The final cutting of that umbilical cord came in AD 70 when, following repeated uprisings among the Jews, the Romans finally lost patience and destroyed the Temple. By then, most of the original apostles and many of the early disciples had died, but not before they had taken the gospel far and wide. Well-supported ancient tradition tells us that Thomas went as far as India, Mark to Egypt, and of course Paul and his companions travelled throughout what today we call Turkey and Greece, Cyprus and Syria, before reaching Rome. Besides these, countless unnamed disciples took the gospel back to their homes throughout the empire and even beyond, or carried it with them as they journeyed on business. They gossiped it in the market place, and wrote it in books and letters. They chatted it in their households, and declared it in the philosophers' debating clubs. They demonstrated it by being better slaves, better wives and mothers and masters, more honest traders, less cruel soldiers.

Wherever they went, they could communicate in the lingua franca of Greek. Women equally with men could follow the call to disciple-making, for the contexts in which it took place were as varied as human life. Eye-witnesses, and those informed by them, quickly captured in writing the stories of Jesus' life and ministry, so that subsequent generations and those too far away to have seen with their own eyes could have a definitive record of what had happened and what the good news was all about. The Gospels were supplemented by the history recorded in Acts – the continuation of "all that Jesus began to do and to teach" (Acts 1:1) – and letters to young churches struggling to work out the implications of their new faith in daily practice. Apostolic teaching could be faithfully transmitted, first orally and soon in writing, in as many places as there were believers.

But, woven through all the bright cloth of those early decades of amazing growth was the persistent thread of weakness and vulnerability. It was costly to be a disciple, and those who sought to bring others into God's family were under no illusion about that. Suffering was normative, not an aberration.

Questions

1. Can you think of some recent examples where the Good News of Jesus has come at "just the right time" for an individual or community? What factors and circumstances helped them hear?

2. How does weakness and vulnerability in Christians aid the spread of the gospel today? How might that affect how we pray for those who suffer?

3. The Great Commission begins with an affirmation of Christ's authority, and ends with the promise of his presence. How does that "fit" with Christians' frequent experience of weakness and suffering when they try to make disciples?

4. What factors in today's world help the spread of the gospel, and what factors hinder it?

6

The Circle Widens

During two hundred and fifty years of sporadic and sometimes severe persecution, the church nonetheless grew and spread. Yet, more and more of its energy was taken up with internal affairs, and it gradually lost its missionary focus. When Constantine became Emperor in AD 312, the church became deeply entwined with political power, with consequences reaching down to the present day.

The Circle Widens

We decided that of the things that are of profit to all mankind, the worship of God ought to be our first and chiefest care, and that it was right that Christians and all others should have freedom to follow the kind of religion they favoured; so that the God who dwells in heaven might be propitious to us and to all under our rule.

Constantine, the Edict of Milan, AD 313

Christ calls those who follow him to be certain that all they do – their "following" – flows from a deep-seated and irrevocable love for the Lord. In this invitation to love him, and out of that love to serve the world, the Christian is invited into the very trinitarian life of God (cf. John 14:11–17).

James Engel/William Dyrness

Nothing can be found in this world more exalted than priests or more sublime than bishops.

Ambrose of Milan (AD 339–397)

"Not by might nor by power, but by my Spirit," says the Lord Almighty.

Zechariah 4:6

Two men sat talking. One came from the state-recognised church, the other from the underground church. The first said, "We are able to be visible, so that people can easily find us; we are allowed a building to meet in, a pastor to lead us, some copies of the Bible. Of course, there are Government controls, but we think we gain more than we lose, we can preach many things, and we are glad to be patriotic." The second replied, "Ah, but we are free! We suffer for our civil disobedience when the authorities find us, but otherwise we are free to love God in our own way. Because it's so hard for us to get Bibles, the Word of God is very precious to us. Unbelievers do not tell us what we may or may not teach." I listened, fascinated. Was either "right" or either "wrong"? Both groups have suffered, and each is vulnerable in different ways. But, both groups have grown, and many true believers are to be found in each. God is building his church!

Confrontation

If weakness was the pervasive experience of the very first era of the church, the picture becomes more ambivalent during the next two centuries. On the one hand, the church continued to grow, numerically and geographically, beginning to make its home in an ever-widening circle of contexts and cultures. On the other, while in some places and at some times persecution intensified and was often very bitter indeed, in other places and at other times the church enjoyed growing prestige and comfort, influence and even wealth.

Along the north coast of Africa, the churches multiplied robustly. To the west, Christianity became firmly established in Spain and Italy. Further north, there were well-documented though still numerically small Christian communities in Gaul (today's southern France), Germany and Britain. These latter three were particularly significant because they represented growth far beyond the boundaries of the Greek-speaking world, and in some cases well beyond the fringes of the Roman empire. This means that by one route and another, Christians must have intentionally travelled past the frontiers of familiar language and culture, and past the relative safety of Rome's orbit, into the precariousness of the unknown. To the east, Armenia and Persia (today's Iran), Ethiopia and India, were all visited by Christians who "planted" churches.

Such progress did not of course go uncontested. Where the

earliest persecution had come at the hands of the Jews, in the second and third centuries it came from pagans, from devotees of the vast pantheon of gods and goddesses venerated around the Mediterranean world, and from time to time from emperors and all the machinery of state. Sometimes it came from philosophers whose empires of the mind were losing credibility. Sometimes it came from those who simply stood to lose money or prestige if the gospel made inroads. Beyond Rome's borders, persecution mostly came as the result of head-on collision with pagan religion or witchcraft and magic.

It would be naïve to suggest that persecution always purified the church. Sometimes it did, discouraging nominal adherents and ensuring a vibrant quality of Christian conviction and life. At other times, trouble led to heresy and apostasy, and some devastating quarrels over how to deal with those who had given way under torture, especially if later they wished to come back within the fold of the church. But, when persecution was at its most bestial, there were remarkable examples of courage and faithfulness, even in the face of martyrdom. Some martyrs preached the gospel fearlessly to the very crowds who had come to watch them torn apart by wild animals, or killed in some other equally brutal manner. Accounts spread widely by word of mouth, and many also were written down and circulated. These stories of bold witness and willingness to die rather than abandon allegiance to Jesus Christ had enormous impact. Many people from all walks of life came to faith as a direct result. Many more, accustomed though they were to brutality, were so sickened by the gratuitous violence against fundamentally good men and women that their loyalty to paganism or to the emperor was undermined.

As the church grew in size and extent, two questions became ever more pressing: how should they keep it from being subverted from within through heresy, and how should they keep all the scattered parts in line with each other? Preoccupation with these issues, critically important though they are, nonetheless made the church increasingly concerned with its structure on the one hand and its internal affairs on the other, to the exclusion of focus on being a missionary community. It was easy, though arguably not wise, to see the answer to be lying in steadily increasing control by ordained leaders, and in implementing a more and more complex organisational structure. Alongside this came more and more detailed legislation, thrashed out in Councils both local and regional, and ironically echoing the Pharisees' explosion of rules. Further, this route of control by power and rules led inexorably to unity being understood in terms of external uniformity rather than in terms of spiritual harmony. Perhaps, had the focus remained outward and missionary, that shared task and objective might have led to unity being understood in very different terms, and subsequent history would have been different.

To be fair, it is not easy to see exactly how they should have tackled the enormous problems they faced, and this same pattern of reaction – a flight into heavy-handed control – has appeared repeatedly down through the centuries. Further, the very Councils whose purpose was to resolve questions and agree on both teaching and practice, came increasingly to be the places where disagreement became most entrenched and from which the fractures of the church would spring. Nonetheless, the slide into dependence on control and power had begun. Increasingly, the Great Commission was taken out of the hands of ordinary disciples and became the concern of the clergy. And those clergy increasingly pursued it through coercion rather than through that human weakness in which God's power can be made perfect.

Alliance with the emperor

In AD 312, Constantine became emperor in the western part of the Roman empire, and a few years later became ruler of the east as well, once more uniting the whole empire under one leader. Because he believed he owed his accession to intervention on his behalf by the Christian God, Constantine first decreed that Christians should be protected rather than persecuted, and later gave them steadily more privileged status. Further, believing that support from the by now sizeable Christian population of his empire was the key to his retaining power (some have suggested that as many as one fifth of his subjects were church members at the time of his accession), Constantine was eager both to win their goodwill towards himself personally and also to deal decisively with divisions within the church. So he introduced many laws which were favourable to Christians, courted them assiduously, and appointed clergy to state responsibilities.

This power was heady stuff, and while one can hardly blame Christians for eagerly grasping respite from the persecution they had endured for so long, they paid a high price for it. Those wishing to ingratiate themselves with Constantine, and observing which way the wind was blowing, decided that it was politic to become Christians. Soon, it was not just politic, it was fashionable. So the church for the first time in its existence was awash with members of nominal faith and little motivation to become committed disciples. Perhaps for the first time, baptism and discipleship became widely uncoupled from each other. That was an enormous, ominous shift from the Great Commission. The church was repeating those dire days of the Old Testament where circumcision became uncoupled from obedience to the Covenant.

This grave development was probably disguised from many Christians as they saw instead the very real advantages of the new system. Thanks to Constantine, they could meet openly without fear of harassment. Their confiscated property was restored to them. Constantine showered the church with money to make multiple copies of the Gospels and other New Testament writings, provided funds to support more clergy, and gave land and money for church buildings and Christian cemeteries. Sundays became public holidays, affording all who wished the opportunity to participate in Christian worship. New laws were announced, in line with Christian values, to protect the vulnerable and to uphold the sanctity of human life. As congregations swelled, all this seemed good news. What Christian wouldn't have gone round with a grin on his face?

Yet the dangerous was intertwined with the good. Clergy life suddenly became rather attractive, and certainly well paid; it was all too easy to be lured by good career prospects rather than to be genuinely called and gifted by God. The multiplication of church buildings detached the propagation of the faith from homes and workplaces and brought it into the much narrower compass of a specialised religious place. Moreover, because of limitations in engineering, church buildings tended to be dark, and increasingly what happened in them came to be focused on what the clergy did at the front while "ordinary" Christians spectated. In the darkness, lit only by a few candles or oil lamps, ill-taught congregations experienced poorly understood mystery instead of the open epiphany of Jesus Christ. Magic, superstition and ignorance were not far behind. The Apostles would have been horrified.

No less horrifying to them would have been Constantine's role in doctrinal discussions. Desperate to have the church united at any price, and with probably only the very haziest of grasps of the niceties of theological debate, Constantine imposed both deadline and outcome on the Council of Nicaea in AD 325. The fourth century saw a series of large and acrimonious Councils, the central issue in all of them being the relationship between the human and divine natures in Christ. Genuine doctrinal differences were complicated by problems with language (how do you express the same truth in languages as different as Latin from Greek?) and cultural context, not to mention personalities. But Constantine set the pattern, to be followed by his successors, that the emperor could dictate to the church and that the key result from each Council must be not truth particularly but structural unity.

This was essential for political stability. And, in an empire increasingly showing internal fault lines, political stability was a high stake to play for. Crucially, Constantine saw Christianity as having a powerful characteristic: unlike any other religion or any other cause, it transcended all national and ethnic boundaries. It had the potential to be the strongest possible "glue" to hold his disparate subjects together. But, only if they were united! Unity at the conclusion of a Council might be (and indeed proved to be) extremely fragile, achieved largely through power struggles rather than through genuine agreement, but from Constantine's point of view it was infinitely better than open warfare. Such "unity" was of course in fact a mockery, and bitter arguments festered and gathered pace. By the end of the fourth century, the Greek-speaking Eastern churches and the by now Latin-speaking Western churches had such deep rifts that substantive reconciliation has never taken place from that day to this. The fragmentation of the church into hostile camps has always, since then, been a major stumbling block for those beyond the frontiers of Christian faith. And, as Constantine correctly foresaw (though for the wrong reasons), the breaking up of the church and the disintegration of the empire were to be inextricably bound up with each other.

It was not only doctrinal divergence or political stability that was at stake. It was also sheer naked power. The bishops and their supporters at various Councils were not above setting about their opponents with stones and staves and fists as they scrambled for their place in the ranking of hierarchy. The church in Rome saw itself as established by the Apostle Peter, to whom, it claimed, had been entrusted the leadership of the church. This trust, they believed, was handed down through the laying on of hands to each succeeding leader of the church in Rome. The bishop of Rome, then, must have superior authority to that of the bishop from anywhere else. When Constantine came to power, this sense of authority being located in Rome was intensified. After all, Rome was the very epicentre of the empire. And, when Constantine moved his palace to Constantinople, the better to keep an eye on the restless east, he even left the bishop of Rome in charge of the city, a dire confusion of spiritual and temporal roles. The Great Commission had explicitly stated that all authority was vested in the Lord Jesus himself, not in one or even all of the disciples; and that, empowered by him and by his Spirit, not by rite or structure, all disciples shared the task of fanning out across the world and making disciples. The fight for supremacy and control, and the emphasis on one location, was a far cry from where the church had started on its mission. Had it not been for Constantine, the domination by the Western Church, and for many centuries specifically by the Roman Catholic Church, would never have been. Whether there would have been greater dialogue and greater humility in relations between the diverging traditions is hard to say. Certainly, the Western Church would have had to operate out of weakness for far longer, and might have been far healthier for it.

Constantine set in motion the process that would lead to the identification of the church with political territory. This came to mean that if a ruler was Christian, then all his subjects must be so, too. This led to mass baptism of whole populations, and vast enforced "conversions". It also led to the practice whereby if a "Christian" king and his armies went to war, and defeated their enemy, all survivors were required to convert. Occasionally a king would be spared if he promised to convert and to have all his people convert. So, it came to be assumed that Christianity should spread through conquest by the sword, and that all inhabitants of territory so won must be baptised into the church. This link between territory and church, and the link in terms of power between church and rulers, came to be called "Christendom".

Alongside all the sub-themes, the greatest legacy of all from Constantine's reign was this enmeshing of church and state. This was decisively to shape the future of the majority of the church for centuries to come, and even to this day still reverberates. As in Constantine's day, the advantageous and the destructive have remained locked together, and have had momentous implications for the fulfilling of the Great Commission ever since. We shall trace glimpses of that complex reality down through the centuries.

Had it not been for the mercy of God, the destructive consequences of this entanglement must have far outweighed the advantageous. Yet, at times, the very interlocking of church and state has, under God, led to great advance; one might argue that case from the rapid expansion during the nineteenth century, for example. At other times, groups of Christians, despairing of the possibility of seeing a spiritual church living in the way it is supposed to live while still shackled to the usually unspiritual machinery of the state, have opted for independency. At other times again, the light of the gospel has been reduced to a mere flicker, where not even any smaller group of believers, whatever its relationship to the state, has seemed to have any impact on the world around it.

Why did not leaders in the church in Constantine's day see the dangers in what was happening? Perhaps some did. It's hard to say. We need to remember that dissent from the powers-that-be was much more difficult then than it is for us in the West today. There was no such thing as democracy, no such thing as human rights, and no such thing as the right of the individual to act independently. Dissent from imperial decrees was punishable by death, and the church was too exhausted after two long centuries of martyrdom to have a death wish. Probably some hoped that in their small corners of the empire, they could go about their business without too much interference provided they didn't make a fuss. Some would have concluded that the advantages outweighed the disadvantages. Some might have recalled the overlap between "church" and state in Israel, and concluded that it was perfectly acceptable.

It is sobering to realise that even the Reformers such as Luther and Calvin, twelve long centuries later, despite the radical nature of their thinking about many issues, did not question the tie between church and state first introduced by Constantine. They, too, believed that a ruler's territory, and the population within it, must submit to his faith. Of course, the important thing then was to ensure that the ruler became Christian, even if by force. This explains the bitter wars of religion that devastated much of Europe for a hundred years in the sixteenth and seventeenth centuries. Moreover, the church must defend at all costs cohesive control over the whole population. Have every newborn child baptised, and it then came automatically under the church's jurisdiction. Let every marriage and every burial come by law under the control of the one territorial church, and the hold over the population was absolute. This is why Calvin was so bitterly opposed to the Anabaptists: they challenged the foundation stones of Christendom. Even the Reformers believed the weight of the state's power should be allied to the church. In three brief centuries, the life-long discipling of the nations which was the passionate legacy of the Lord Jesus had been subverted to the administration of certain rites of passage, in which radical new lifestyle, repentance and faith, might not figure at all. The imposition of a religion had replaced the costly embracing of a Saviour.

The question of church–state relationships has become increasingly pressing in recent centuries, yet it was only towards the end of the twentieth century that for much of the worldwide church the assumptions of Christendom have finally been shown to be untenable. The Orthodox Church, and to a lesser extent the Roman Catholic Church, still operate a system of territorialism whereby other branches of the Christian family are unwelcome in "their" historic lands and close links with the political powers are fostered. Sometimes, at a very pragmatic level, this may appear to have facilitated the survival of the church in a hostile setting, for example, in Russia under Communism. Certainly, a territorial church may nurture a sense of national identity during dark days, and lead to popular uprisings, as in Poland in the 1980s, which challenge unjust governments. But, when a territorial church lives in a context of greater political stability and freedom, the same problems that quickly appeared in Constantine's day all too readily appear again. Temporal power and wealth are very seductive. They make a church complacent, and suck from it its spiritual vitality. Not least, they do that because, if everyone in the country is "Christian", the church is taken up with maintenance and loses sight of its God-given mission. The advantage of weakness is that you know you desperately need the grace of God.

But, there have always been some who have turned their backs on the Christendom model and chosen another route. It is to them that we now turn.

Questions

1. What are some of the temptations to ally with worldly power that we succumb to today?
2. What are some of the advantages and some of the problems associated with territorial/Constantinian model churches today?
3. How can we respond firmly to heresy and divisions without resorting to heavy-handed leadership?
4. How do language and culture differences make it hard for Christians to get along with each other? What can we do about it?

7

Rebels – or Heirs of the Apostles?

For many centuries, the monastic orders were at the heart of the expansion of the church. They crossed frontiers of language and culture to carry the Christian message to new communities. And, in a variety of ways, they set about discipling those to whom they went.

Rebels – or Heirs of the Apostles?

I was a free man in a good position, and I bargained away my noble status – and I am not ashamed of this or regretful about it – for the sake of others. In short, I am a slave of Christ in a remote country because of the unspeakable glory of eternal life which is in Christ Jesus our Lord.

Patrick of Ireland (c.AD 389–c.AD 461)

Pour into their untaught minds the preaching of both the Old and the New Testaments in the spirit of virtue and love and sobriety and with reasoning suited to their understanding.

Boniface, English missionary to Germany (c.AD 680–c.AD 754)

O Lord our God, grant us grace to desire you with our whole heart; that so desiring, we may seek, and seeking, find you; and so finding you, may love you; and loving you, may hate those sins from which you have redeemed us.

Anselm of Canterbury (1033–1109)

I sat with a very old lady, hovering on the brink of heaven. Once immensely active, now she was confined to one room, rarely able to move beyond bed or chair. Perhaps reading my unspoken thoughts, and with bright eyes twinkling, she gently said, "Don't pity me! I am having such a good time! When I lie awake at night, or sit here for many hours each day on my own, I can travel the world in my prayers. I used to think, 'What a waste!' about monastic life. But now I realise what a lovely privilege it is to be 'devoted to prayer'. I've learnt so much more about God's love and longing for the world. Now, tell me about X and Y so that I can pray for them!" I went home thinking, "Thank you, Lord, for such beautiful missionary service from a 93-year-old!"

Missionary monks

Around the warm, dry eastern end of the Mediterranean, for centuries before Christ, men (and very occasionally women) sometimes chose to withdraw into the desert to pursue spiritual enlightenment away from the distractions of ordinary life. In the Jewish tradition, some of the prophets had done that for periods of time, recharging their batteries before another uphill tussle with their usually apostate fellow-countrymen. John the Baptist's desert sojourn would thus have been entirely comprehensible to his contemporaries, whether or not they liked what he had to say as a result, and the Lord Jesus' forty days in the wilderness would have been regarded as a natural precursor to his public ministry.

Mostly, these men lived on their own – after all, solitude was the condition by which they believed they would find what they sought – but occasionally a group would find adjacent caves to live in, thus softening the sharpness of entirely solitary life while preserving the benefits. Even more rarely still, a community would live together in some remote place, with the specific purpose of devoting themselves to the religious life.

So, it was perhaps inevitable that before long this pattern should be adopted and adapted by the Christian church, or at least by a handful of Christians, who soon became a great army. The Christian monastic movement had begun. It was to have enormous significance for the development of the church, and became one of the most important means of evangelising and discipling new regions. It is even arguable that the missionary societies which sprung up in the nineteenth and twentieth centuries, in the enormous energy of the Protestant missionary movement, were – albeit unconsciously – modelled on earlier monastic orders.

At first, a small handful of Christians disappeared into the desert purely and simply to deal with their own souls. They weren't interested in anybody else's, but couldn't cope with living what they understood to be the Christian life in the context of the noise and corruption of society. They didn't consider that the church lived the way it should, either, and they could attain loftier heights of spirituality away from it than within it. Mind you, even the most bizarre of these people sometimes became tourist attractions and came to be evangelists in the most unlikely ways. It is said that Simeon Stylites, who retreated to the top of a lofty pillar, bawled the gospel down to those who came to gawp. Antony in Egypt was frequently consulted by church leaders for his wise and spiritual advice. It's easy to dismiss these folk as cranks, or as having personality disorders (or possibly only disagreeable relatives to be escaped from), but the evidence seems much more complex than that. They were taking a recognised religious pattern, and recasting it within the Christian faith.

Specifically Christian monastic communities sprang up around the time Constantine came to power, in the early fourth century. The earliest of these were founded by Pachomius in Egypt, Basil in Cappadocia (modern Turkey), and Martin of Tours in France. Pachomius and Martin had both been soldiers before embarking on the monastic life, and each brought to their communities the disciplined lifestyle drilled into them by some sergeant-major in their past. This both delivered them from the excesses of asceticism (for example, fasting to the point of emaciation or hallucination), and also gave voluntary communal life a clear structure of order and obedience, along with celibacy.

Basil's distinctive was to use his monastery as the base for serving and discipling the local community. He saw monastic life as the way of resourcing a group of Christians to teach and heal and tend the poor. Martin, on the other hand, vowed that wherever the armies of Rome had gone to conquer in the cause of imperial splendour, his monks would go, pair by pair, to capture people's hearts in the cause of the King of kings and his far greater glory. His order was unashamedly missionary in intention, and all that happened in his monasteries revolved around that fundamental purpose.

It was to Tours that Patrick came in the early fifth century. Almost certainly, he came as an escapee from slavery in Ireland, whither he had been taken as a captive from the British mainland. Exactly how or why he came to Tours we do not know, though Brittany shared Ireland's Celtic culture. What we do know is that, along with copying precious Gospel manuscripts, Patrick imbibed Martin's passionate missionary vision. Before long, the refugee returned to the Ireland from which he'd fled, this time with the determination to plant the gospel.

Patrick's return was significant in more ways than the blessing it brought to Ireland. He was going beyond the furthest point the Romans had ever reached in the west. And he was a monk, a missionary-minded monk at that, going beyond the farthest point the Roman church had ever reached. Others before him had gone from Tours beyond the northern boundaries of the empire, and had established Christian communities outside the Roman system. Now Patrick was to do the same in Ireland.

Whether through inspiration or through force of circumstances, Patrick's strategy was not to plant diocesan churches (there were after all no Roman administrative units, or dioceses, to use) but to disciple into being tiny monastic communities in the territories of each tribal lord. Where Pachomius and Basil and the others had established their monasteries alongside – almost supplementary to – the local churches, Patrick's monasteries *were* the church. These communities then became the base of discipling the local population and of further missionary outreach. It was at the monasteries that converts would gather for worship, to have their babies baptised, their young people married, their dead buried. The by now traditional skills of the monasteries – copying Scripture, nursing the sick, dealing with witchcraft, teaching Bible stories – were supplemented by bringing into the community the young sons of local chieftains and leaders. Some would themselves become monks, others would return to life outside the monastery, but, in the latter case, they would often be strong advocates for the Christian cause.

Patrick's ministry led to the flowering of what came to be called "Celtic Christianity". It was not especially antagonistic towards Roman Christianity, just outside it, and developing in a manner more appropriate to its setting. There had been some Christian activity among Celtic people long before Patrick arrived on the scene, but it was his work that gave the impetus to a great missionary movement which lasted for more than 150 years. From Ireland, missionaries went to Scotland and also back to the European continent. Then, missionaries from Scotland went to the north of England, as well as to Europe. They repeated the effective pattern adopted by Patrick: send out monks in pairs or small groups, establish a tiny community as a bridgehead, win over a chieftain, establish a church, send out monks. . . The missionary vision embedded at the very heart of Celtic Christian faith took monks to France and Switzerland, to Germany and Holland and beyond.

The Celtic monasteries became centres of scholarship as well as of mission. Some of the most famous early, beautifully illuminated copies of the Gospels were their work. They also developed a distinctive spirituality, associated to this day with places such as Iona and Lindisfarne, where mind and emotion joined hands, and where the raw wild beauty of the setting of many of their monasteries led to a profound reverence for Creator and creation.

Tragically, the death blow for Celtic Christianity, with all its vigour and vision, was struck by fellow Christians. The Roman church could not tolerate a church system that did not come under its control, and when Roman and Celtic Christianity came nose to nose in the north of England in AD 664 it was the beginning of the end. The issues debated at the Synod of

Whitby varied from the absurd (which parts of a monk's head should be shaved bald) through the comparatively minor (how you set the date of Easter). Actually, the head shaving bit had important cultural, symbolic meaning for the Celts, which the Roman church leaders refused to acknowledge; and the bishop of Rome, still smarting from being worsted in an argument with the Eastern churches over the dating of Easter, was determined to knock the Celts into (his) line rather than be humiliated again.

But behind it all the issues were really about power and control: whose word was final? If you were the bishop of Rome, could you permit churches that did not come under the direct control of a diocesan bishop? The diocesan bishop system nicely tracked ultimate authority back to yourself. . . The Roman bishops had armies to back them up, and, intimidated, local kings who had happily lived under the Celtic system, felt bound to capitulate. The Roman church had come to power under Constantine and learned its lessons of imperialism well.

The bright flame of Celtic Christianity was extinguished, and with it the missionary impetus went, too. All too soon, Viking raiders were to over-run both Celtic and Roman church strongholds, pillaging, burning, destroying. Britain once more plunged into pagan darkness.

It was all a long way from Calvary, and a long way from a little group of Spirit-dependent disciples. Simple, tenacious love for the Master had given way to addiction to control.

To the ends of the earth

Monks and monasteries (and their female counterparts, nuns and convents) have tended to have rather bad press in Protestant circles. To be sure, there were things that went badly awry in some monasteries at some points in history and in some places. That was especially true where monasteries gathered power and land and wealth, all of which have the potential to be profoundly corrupting, no matter whose hands they are in. The worst of the monasteries were very bad indeed, but on the other hand, the best were extremely valuable, not least in taking the gospel into new areas.

But Protestant perceptions of the monastic movement have at least been massaged by those with vested interests. Henry VIII happily exploited some genuine grievances against the monasteries to justify looting and destroying them. It suited his greed very well, as well as wiping out one group who dared to challenge his actions. Only later did ordinary people wake up to the fact that they had lost, along with the monasteries, their main provider of schooling for their young and care for their sick. The Reformers were also opposed to the monasteries (though Luther, for example, in fact owed a very great deal to his). It is hard not to conclude that the real reason for their opposition was not simply outrage at the abuses to be found in some. Rather, they needed to dismantle any structure that could retain loyalty to the Pope or act in parallel to the churches, and thus undermine their own control. They were also rightly anxious to dispel the myth that it was only through monastery or convent life that a man or woman could achieve real spiritual stature, that the laity were somehow spiritually inferior.

However that may be, the monasteries at their best were crucial to the survival of the church. They were the chief places where Scriptures could be found and copied and studied, and where every kind of scholarship was protected. They produced preachers and teachers, and in some cases those who then explained the Christian faith in the local languages rather than in Latin. They demonstrated practical Christian compassion as they taught the young and cared for the sick and the poor. Whenever the church lapsed into corruption, it was from the monasteries that reformers and protesters mainly came, and many times it was these monks and nuns who brought spiritual light and life back into the Christian enterprise.

And, always, the best of the monasteries retained a missionary vision. It was Francis of Assisi in the thirteenth century, and later Raymond Lull of the Franciscan order founded by Francis, who attempted peaceable evangelisation among the Muslims. Islam had swept through North Africa, Palestine and Syria, and many of the earlier heartlands of Christianity, and soon through much of Europe as well. Apart from the Franciscans' attempt to enter into civilised dialogue, the church's response was to engage in the increasingly bestial Crusades, where both sides excelled themselves in brutal slaughter. From that day to this, fairly or unfairly (since Muslims were quite as violent), the memory of the Crusades has made significant evangelism among Muslims impossible, and one wonders what might have been had the church listened more carefully to Francis and Lull. More happily, it was monks who penetrated the fierce peoples of Scandinavia; over in the east, Orthodox monks had a vital role in establishing the church in Russia; and Nestorian monks travelled all the way into eastern China.

But it was perhaps the Jesuits who became the most remarkable missionary order of all. Founded in 1540 by Ignatius Loyola, the Jesuits' *raison d'être* from the start was to take the Christian faith to the ends of the earth. And the ends of the earth were expanding dramatically, as Spanish and Portuguese sailors in particular sailed into the unknown and "discovered" new continents: North America, South America, sub-Saharan Africa, and great chunks of Asia. They faced appalling danger as their little boats were tossed and strained across vast oceans. But, apart from the adrenalin of the born adventurer, there were huge prizes for those who succeeded. The Spanish and Portuguese crowns were at the height of their powers, and were eager to spread their empires around the globe. Some monarchs were truly devout, others saw the political advantages in putting the Pope in their debt. Either way, they were very happy to have monks and priests sail along, too.

There are, of course, great moral problems about incorporating unwilling native populations into the church at sword-point, especially where the church becomes the key agent for keeping them in submission to the invader. Here is a desperately painful application of the Christendom concept. Yet it is clear that many of the Jesuits genuinely wished to bring these newly-discovered peoples into the fold of the church, and believed that the end – their eternal well-being once they were safely baptised – justified the means. In some cases, the monks and priests intervened to prevent wholesale slaughter of native people by the soldiers and fortune-seekers who also crowded the little boats. These were the men who established settlements from which to grab the gold and silver, spices and slaves to take to a hungry market back home. It was usually the monks and priests who stood between the sheer unbridled greed of their compatriots, safe in the possession of gunpowder, and the bewildered, unarmed local people.

Within fifteen years of the foundation of the order, the Jesuits numbered over a thousand, and within eighty years there were nearly sixteen thousand, a highly committed, disciplined and formidable missionary task force. Such growth is impressive by any measurement. This was especially the case given that training was lengthy and rigorous (up to fifteen years) and the conditions in which the members worked usually very hard and often dangerous. Their training stood them in good stead, and they often became brilliant linguists and translators, gifted teachers, and acute observers of cultures. Further, their training, based on Loyola's "Spiritual Exercises", taught them spiritual disciplines to nourish spiritual life in any circumstances. Wherever they went, they discipled as they themselves had been discipled, deliberately and comprehensively, and yet also showed a profounder sensitivity to cultural context than almost any Christian group before them and many since. Frequently, they set up villages around a simple church and a school, and made the whole of life revolve around these. They developed a pattern which integrated faith with every part of every day's activity. Everybody, child and adult, was drilled into memorising the catechism, a creed, prayers, and portions of Scripture. Where it was possible so to do, in time they established schools and universities to the highest standards, seeking thereby to inculcate Christian faith into those they perceived to be the upcoming leaders of society.

It is no accident that some of the Jesuits are famous to this day, even to those who do not share their particular form of Christian faith. Some, like Francis Xavier, are remembered for their astonishing pioneering not in one country but several, in Xavier's case in India, Malaysia and Vietnam, Indonesia and Japan. He died attempting China. In each of these, he established churches which have survived to the present, and many of the foundations he laid are still effective. Matteo Ricci immersed himself in Chinese language and culture, and was greatly respected by Chinese scholars. This was remarkable in a day when China was profoundly hostile to foreigners. Finally, Ricci was able to spend the last ten years of his life in Peking (Beijing), where his knowledge of astronomy and of clocks won him imperial favour. By the time he died, about 2,000 had been baptised in Peking, and within thirty years of his death there may have been as many as a quarter of a million Catholic Christians in China.

Ricci worked hard at finding appropriate ways of expressing the Christian message and lifestyle in a Chinese context. Many years later, Franciscans and Dominicans accused Ricci of having gone too far in accommodating certain elements of Chinese culture, and eventually this and other matters led to the Jesuits falling into papal disfavour for a time. Yet, Ricci was struggling with a crucial issue. What should the gospel look like, and what should the church look like, in a setting so radically different from his European home country? If the early church had to come to terms with the fact that Gentiles did not have to become Jews to become Christians, surely it was wrong to ask the Chinese to become pseudo-Europeans? In what ways did Chinese culture reflect the fact that even as pagans these were men and women created in the image of God? What could be affirmed and what must be rejected? What parts of Chinese culture were just neutral, and could be invested with new Christian meaning?

Whether or not Ricci reached the right conclusions, he was certainly addressing the right questions. Interestingly enough, the issues which especially taxed him, for example, how to respond to ancestor practices, are still issues about which Christians in Asia debate today. And issues of "critical contextualisation" – being faithful to God's truth yet relevant to a different culture – still stretch the best missionary minds in our generation.

Did the Jesuits and the rest conquer the world for Christ, for the Pope, for their monarchs? Perhaps all three are tangled together. Yet, the monastic orders undoubtedly pushed out the geographical boundaries of the church in an amazing way. Since the Protestant Reformation of the sixteenth century, Roman Catholic orders of both men and women have had an unbroken record of missionary service. They have often worked among the poorest of the poor. Mother Teresa of Calcutta, a tiny Albanian nun, became arguably one of the best-known figures of the twentieth century; around the world people of all faiths and none admired what she did and noted that she did it in the name of Jesus Christ. In Latin America, India, China and the Philippines, nuns in particular have been instrumental in bringing renewal into the Roman Catholic church in the past half century.

With very few exceptions, the Protestants did not re-establish monastic orders. Yet, when the Protestant missionary movement finally gathered momentum in the nineteenth century, many missionary societies developed characteristics similar to those of the monastic movements they had been trained to be suspicious of. But that's another story.

Questions

1. What lessons can we learn from the monastic orders of the past, both as inspiration and as warning?
2. How might some of the basic concepts of the monastic model(s) be adapted for use today?
3. How can we disciple our children without falling into "the cross and the sword" trap?
4. Some forms of spirituality developed by the monastic orders, including Celtic spirituality, have become popular again in the West. However, they are almost always now detached from the passionate missionary vision at the heart of their original form. Why do you think this is?

8

The Church of a Thousand Streams

With the coming of the Reformation in the sixteenth century, Western Christianity split into more and more streams. Different branches of Protestantism had very different approaches to mission among those outside their own communities, and even to discipling those within.

The Church of a Thousand Streams

Say among the nations, "The Lord reigns . . ." He will judge the world in righteousness, and the peoples in his truth.

Psalm 96:10,13

I stand convicted by the Scriptures to which I have appealed, and my conscience is taken captive by God's word, I cannot and will not recant anything. For to act against conscience is neither safe for us nor open to us. On this I take my stand. I can do no other. God help me. Amen.

Martin Luther (1483–1546)

What is the chief end of man? Man's chief end is to glorify God and to enjoy him for ever.

From *The Westminster Confession (1647)*

My heaven is to please God and glorify him, and to give all to him, and to be wholly devoted to his glory; that is the heaven I long for.

David Brainerd (1718–1747)

O for a thousand tongues to sing
my great Redeemer's praise,
the glories of my God and King,
the triumphs of His grace!

My gracious Master, and my God,
assist me to proclaim,
to spread through all the earth abroad
the honours of Thy name.

Charles Wesley (1707–1788)

Not far from where I live, there are four churches, one on each corner of the same crossroads. Each claims to preach the gospel (and probably does). Each has a small, struggling congregation whose energies (and wallets) are largely taken up with keeping the roof in good enough order to withstand our fierce weather, and just keeping going. In the surrounding estates, probably 95% of the people never set foot in any kind of church, and know next to nothing about Jesus Christ.

Once, I lived in an Asian city where there were more than forty different imported Baptist denominations, and as many again home-grown ones. You wouldn't think there could be that many kinds of Baptist, would you? Meanwhile, most of the population had no idea what the gospel is really all about.

It's head-scratching stuff.

Starting again?

Luther was not the first to try to bring badly needed reform into the church. In fact he was just one in a long line of reformers, many of them, like himself, nurtured within the monastic tradition. But, the events of 1517 and thereafter brought irrevocable change to the Western church, shattering it into many distinct parts. Along with enormous energy and genuine spiritual renewal, there were also some less positive outcomes. And, of course, there were the political opportunists who exploited the Reformation for their own far from godly ends.

From this distance, it is not difficult to identify some of the great blessings that came through the Reformation as well as some of the weaknesses. There was an explosion of vernacular translations of the Bible, making it available to people in their own language instead of the Latin they did not understand. The recent invention of the printing press made it possible for multiple copies of the Scriptures, along with a torrent of other Christian literature, to be produced. Thus, for instance, for the first time it became practicable for a copy of the Bible to be installed in every church in England. In theory at least, and frequently in practice, it was much more likely that ordinary folk could hear the gospel of grace, that they wouldn't be exploited financially in some vain quest to buy God's favour, and that they could recapture the immediacy of being able to deal with God directly rather than through the mediation of a priest. These, and much more, were no small gains, and we should never lose sight of that.

Nonetheless, it would be arrogant and ignorant to suggest that overnight all that was wrong with the church was swept away, and that Protestantism recaptured all the strengths and none of the shortcomings of the New Testament church. Perhaps most of all, the Apostles would have been dismayed that despite all that vigour and emphasis upon the gospel, and the colossal theological enterprise, there was next to no attention paid to the Great Commission. The reasons for this were manifold, and here we can only give the sketchiest of outlines. But it is important that we see why there was this enormous blank spot when so much vital New Testament doctrine was being reinstated at the heart of this new river of the church.

For more than a century after Luther's fateful posting of his ninety-five theses on the door of the church at Wittenberg, Europe descended into ever more bloody war. Sometimes it was between Roman Catholic and Protestant states, sometimes between Protestant and Protestant, and sometimes it was the especial tragedy of civil war between warring factions within a state. Nation after nation was torn apart, populations decimated, land laid waste, coffers emptied. It produced both exhaustion and cynicism about the church, to be tragically repeated in the twentieth century when another round of wars between allegedly Christian nations once more brought the gospel into disrepute. Few people had the strength or energy to care about the world beyond their own horizons. The rapid, bitter fragmentation of Protestantism exacerbated the focus on self-preservation rather than mission.

Further, the towering giants of the Reformation – Luther, Calvin, Zwingli and Knox – had very little to say about the Great Commission. On the whole, they believed that the missionary mandate had been given specifically to the Apostles and did not apply, at least not in any recognisably similar way, to the church in their own day. If the office of Apostle had died out with the original holders, then certain responsibilities of apostleship, such as transmitting Scripture or defining the boundaries of the Christian enterprise, must have died out with them. This argument was patently inconsistent with their insistence that other parts of the apostolic task were still binding on the church, but it was their sincere belief.

None of them questioned the basic assumptions of Christendom. They believed strongly in territorial churches, whereby all those who lived in a given state must be treated as being within the church of that state. Who, then, if everybody was already "inside", was there to be treated as "outside"? Rather, their energy must focus on reforming the church structures, procedures and teaching, so that everybody should come under the kind of church discipline which swept away nominalism and fostered serious Christian living. Some people of the day sadly believed that those with differently coloured skin, and beyond European "civilisation", were not fully human and probably, unlike themselves, not destined by God for eternal life. Christendom was the evidence of God's election of a superior race. Had he wished to include others in the blessings of the gospel, then they would have been included long ago and the early church would have spread to those regions as well. These arguments, too, are inconsistent and untenable, but had we lived then we might have shared those ideas.

Others again so stressed the sovereignty of God that they washed their hands of human responsibility in reaching the unreached of the world. As late as the end of the eighteenth century, when William Carey was urging his fellow ministers to adopt "means" – planned action – to evangelise the world, his moderator is reputed to have said, "Sit down, young man! If God intended to take the gospel to the heathen, he would do it without your help or mine." Certainly the church needed to recover a deep sense of the sovereign Lordship of Christ, too often eclipsed by the apparent ultimate power of the church's temporal leaders. But divine sovereignty and human responsibility are to be held in balance, not one at the expense of the other.

It was perhaps most of all the Reformers' understanding of the church which stood in the way of their putting mission at the heart of its life in any practical way. Apart from their understanding of Christendom which we have already noted, they believed the pastor and teacher to be the key roles within the church. But neither the pastor nor the teacher is focused primarily on the unbeliever. While the pastor-teacher gifts are vital for discipling those already within the church family, they do not necessarily bring people in in the first place, and don't deal with the issues of pioneering in unevangelised communities. Or do they? Some would argue that the proper teaching of God's word is always evangelistic, that is, bearing the message of the gospel, as well as being the means of nurturing God's people.

The Reformers' understanding of the church meant that they simply could not accommodate what today are often called "para-church" movements, that is, specially focused task groups which do not fall under the direction of the local church or its denominational structure. We have already seen how for centuries the monastic orders rather than local congregations had provided the main vehicle through which mission among the unevangelised happened. In abolishing rather than reforming the monasteries and orders, the Reformers destroyed the only contemporary model for engaging in mission beyond the frontiers.

Lastly, the Reformers did not really "give the Church back to the laity". For centuries, the people had been mainly spectators (and the source of money). Priests and other "professionals" were the only ones who could perform the rites and do the real business. In theory, Protestantism was supposed to dismantle priestcraft and make it possible for ordinary men and women to play a full part in the life of the churches. In some places, especially where lay people were well educated or of high social standing, this happened. But for the greater majority the change must have been a pious theory only. Those in charge found it hard to trust the Spirit of God at work in those less well educated than themselves, a problem that was to plague the Protestant missionary thrust into Africa and Asia and Latin America of three centuries later. To be fair, this was in large measure simply a reflection of social organisation, and Protestantism did increasingly though very gradually lead to a more democratic society. Nonetheless, one of the major geniuses of the New Testament church was that regardless of social standing (remember, many of the early Christians were slaves) every believer was expected to play their part in discipling others. The Reformation churches did not recapture this vital principle, and there is little evidence that the Reformers expected it of them.

The mainstream Reformation was, under God, a highly significant stage in the life of the Christian church. Nonetheless, it was left to groups outside the mainstream to pick up the torch of mission.

Beyond the fringe

Despite their failure to question the concept of Christendom, the Reformers never quite worked out how the various churches that quickly emerged should relate to each other. So, uneasily, the principles of Christendom came to be applied within a sovereign territory rather than producing one coherent Protestant church over a wider area. There was plenty of squabbling between them, and sometimes open warfare, as, for example in the terrible confrontation between Luther and Zwingli over precisely what happened in the Eucharist.

One thing, however, they were agreed on, and that was that a plurality of systems – which we today would call denominations – was absolutely not to be allowed. That, after all, was incompatible with the fundamentals of Christendom. In one state there must be one church dealing with one state authority, be that king or prince or council. So when, in Switzerland in 1525, a small group broke away from the reform movement in Zurich and "went independent", reaction was swift and deadly. The rebels, who came to be called Anabaptists, had two main claims. Firstly, they said that the city Council were not implementing the decisions of the reforming church fast enough, and therefore the link between church and state should be broken. Secondly, they said that the routine baptism of infants led to nominalism, and that baptism should be on profession of personal faith by adults committed to take their discipleship seriously.

We are so familiar with this position today that we may be puzzled as to why it caused such a violent reaction. But it was the undermining of the one church's authority in any given state that was the issue. For centuries, there had been one church throughout the West. Now the genie was out of the bottle, and what had begun as a desire to bring reform from within that one church was rapidly heading towards fragmentation on a scale that could not be countenanced. The first real cracks in the pattern of Christendom, the paradigm of twelve hundred years, had appeared.

The Anabaptist movement hung doggedly on, and though many gave their lives for their convictions their experience of being a small persecuted group rapidly led to them becoming a missionary movement. They believed themselves to be right, and that all around them were people who needed not so much to be pastored as if they were believers as to be brought to faith in the first place. As in the early church, persecution scattered them. They went out in twos and threes, systematically throughout Europe, in order to urge people to come to personal commitment to Jesus Christ, with (re)baptism as the outward sign of that commitment, and to urge active discipleship.

Many of the little groups that came into being through their work were slaughtered by the local powers, be they Roman Catholic or Protestant. But three survived. The best known of these was the Mennonite community, who later migrated from Holland to North America in search of peace and freedom. Less well known, but more significant for our present story, was the Hutterite community, who for a long time found refuge on the estate of a sympathetic aristocrat in Moravia, thus earning the name "the Moravians".

In 1727, two hundred years after the Anabaptists began, the by now very motley collection of refugees in the Moravian community came quarrelling and fighting to the Lord's table. God met with them in such an overwhelming way that they likened it to experiencing Pentecost with the early church. Reconciled with one another, and with a profound sense of calling, they embarked on a missionary movement whose impact far outweighed their numbers. They claimed that it was not possible to experience the power of the Spirit in such a way and not devote themselves to the Great Commission. It was to be Moravian missionaries, first on board ship to Georgia and later in London, who were to bring John Wesley to assurance of faith. Wesley in his turn became one of the great missionaries of the eighteenth century to the unevangelised masses of England. Anabaptist, and Moravian, experience of persecution had led them to put great stress on interdependent life in small tight-knit communities. This influenced Wesley to develop the Methodist class system, where all converts were assigned to small groups, or "classes". This proved to be one of the most effective models of discipling Christians ever seen in the history of the church. It should not surprise us. It is after all closely modelled on our Lord's strategy with his chosen twelve.

Another group to fall foul of Christendom were the Puritans. Originally a group within the Church of England, their desire to press reform far beyond what was acceptable either to the crown or to the bishops inevitably led most to independency. Others remained Anglican, but could not contemplate staying in a setting they so passionately disapproved: Anglican at a safe distance, but not here. As persecution intensified, they finally emigrated in large numbers to North America. It was a brave move, and their wistfulness for their unforgiving homeland was betrayed in the names they gave their new settlements: New England, New Hampshire, Boston, New York, Plymouth. But, brave though it was, we should be under no illusion as to their motive in going. They did not go in order to engage in mission among the heathen; they more frequently killed the native population than sought to convert them. They went because they wanted freedom to pursue their faith in the way their conscience dictated. Soon they were to discover that their conscience was not quite as united as they had hoped, and before long they, too, were breaking apart into acrimonious groups.

They set out to build thorough-going Christian communities, "the new Jerusalem on earth", and were dismayed that it didn't work out that way. Even Puritans, they discovered, struggled with human fallenness. They longed for the fullness of the kingdom here and now, and their beliefs about the end of the world and the Lord's return encouraged them. In their eagerness to grasp the impossible, they sometimes could not see the difference between loving discipling and ruthless discipline. Their passionate commitment to root out sin sometimes led to tragedy, as in the infamous witchcraft trials. Sadly, recent research suggests that probably those who were accused of demon possession, and burnt or drowned, may have been victims of mouldy rye, a chemical in which causes hallucinations and fits. In trying to purge their communities, they built walls which excluded those who didn't measure up to their standards rather than coping with the messy business of mission.

The Puritans illustrate important issues that have been problematic for the church down through the centuries and have often dogged its struggles to obey the Great Commission. How pure (and doctrinally "sound") must a church be to be called a church? What is the role of individual conscience? How do you resolve the impasse when different but equally committed Christians cannot agree about how to interpret and apply this teaching of Scripture or that? How can a Christian community combine a passion for holiness with loving overtures to the sinner? What does it mean that the kingdom of God has come already, and in what sense must it always be future until the end of time? These are deep questions which have always faced the people of God, whether or not they have been aware of it.

It would not be right to leave the Puritans on that negative note, for in the grace of God they brought great enrichment to the church, too. They produced some fine thinkers and writers, whose work is still inspirational, deeply rooted in Scripture, fragrant with the love of God. At their best, they demonstrate for all time what it means to love the Lord Jesus Christ with mind and body and soul. Some among them grew to have a passionate heart for the native American Indian peoples, and risked their lives to bring the gospel to them. And the Puritan movement in time fed into the Great Awakening, which in turn influenced Wesley and Whitefield; and Wesley and Whitefield's ministry in the mission fields of Britain was to inspire a humble cobbler-pastor called William Carey. And William Carey was to be used by God to change the face of the world.

Questions

1. How does hostility between different streams of the church hinder the cause of the Great Commission?
2. How can we discern which movements "beyond the fringe" are truly works of God and which are not?
3. In what ways might Christians from different streams of the church work more effectively together to reach those outside?
4. Why was Wesley's "class system" so effective in discipling young believers? How might we adapt and incorporate that today?

9

Protestants Wake Up: for Christ or Empire?

The nineteenth century is sometimes called "The Great Century" as far as the expansion of the church is concerned. The modern missionary movement swelled into life alongside the swift growth of Protestant Europe's political empires and America's overflowing energy. By the century's end, and often involving great sacrifice, there were bridgeheads for the gospel in many parts of the world.

Protestants Wake Up: for Christ or Empire?

> The rich man in his castle,
> the poor man at his gate,
> God made them, high or lowly,
> and order'd their estate.
> > *Cecil Frances Alexander (1818–1895)*

Expect great things from God. Attempt great things for God.
> *William Carey (1761–1834)*

Those two pioneers of civilisation – Christianity and commerce – should ever be inseparable.
> *David Livingstone (1813–1873)*

If I had a thousand lives, I would give them all for the women of China.
> *Lottie Moon (1840–1912)*

If as an act of obedience we were to determine that every district, every town, every village, every hamlet in this land should hear the gospel, and that speedily, and were to set about doing it, I believe the Spirit would come down in such mighty power that we would find supplies springing up we know not how. We should find the fire spreading from missionary to flock, and our native fellow-workers and the whole Church of God would be blessed. God gives his Holy Spirit to them that obey him.
> *James Hudson Taylor (1832–1905)*

China is not to be won for Christ by quiet, ease-loving men and women. . . The stamp of men and women we need is such as will put Jesus, China, souls, first and foremost in everything and at every time – even life itself must be secondary. . . Of such men, and such women, do not fear to send us too many. They are more precious than rubies.

James Hudson Taylor (1832–1905)

Tucked away in a quiet corner of the burial ground was an area given over to foreigners. It was poignant to stand there knowing that many of the graves, marked and unmarked, contained the remains of missionary men and women. And all the little graves! How many missionary children died! I thought of the Lord Jesus' words, "I tell you the truth, unless a kernel of wheat falls to the ground and dies, it remains only a single seed. But if it dies, it produces many seeds." Well, in this country there had certainly been years of sowing with many tears – the best part of a century before there was any sign of appreciable harvest. But now, at last it seems the time for reaping has come. As I turned away, I thought that perhaps in heaven that day, those men and women and children were rejoicing side by side with men and women and children from this land where they had given their lives for love of the Lord Jesus. They did not see the harvest in their lifetime, but God keeps his promises: it has surely come.

The ambiguity of strength

If the Reformation was to throw into relief some of the inconsistencies of Christendom, the nineteenth and early twentieth centuries were to witness a new flowering of the same mind-set, albeit with new permutations. Once upon a time, Christendom had been Constantine's empire. Then, it had become the domain of the Roman church, encompassing mostly what today we call Western Europe. Later still, depending on your point of view, it became Roman Catholic territories wherever they were in the world, or alternatively Protestant territories, almost all of which were in northern and western Europe plus the east part of America. Of course, the Orthodox family of churches had their own views on the matter, too. But, whichever camp you belonged to, and however vaguely understood, the link between land and state and church was not questioned by most people in the "Christian" world. Being Christian was less a matter of active discipleship, more a matter of where you were born and lived.

By the early nineteenth century, Protestant countries in particular had become rather smug about the perceived entire superiority of their culture(s). Few could distinguish in any way between their way of life (which had, of course, been considerably influenced by centuries of Christianity) and the Christian faith itself, even if they paid at least lip service to it. There had been an explosion of scientific discovery and industrial development, and steadily through the century the conviction grew that human reason and human effort, nurtured in the cradle of Western civilisation, could not help but transform the whole human race. The modern scientific enterprise had had its roots in the Christian faith, seeking to uncover the laws that the Creator had established in his creation, but by now God had become largely superfluous: humankind, especially the Protestant variety, was perfectly capable of running the world. Christian discipleship had been reduced to a cultural veneer.

It was in this philosophical context that the British empire expanded over several continents. There were, of course, other Protestant countries (Germany, for example) also collecting empires, but it was Britain above all that controlled more and more of the world. Sore at losing her American colonies, pride dictated she compensate elsewhere. If you were philanthropic, or even genuinely Christian, you assumed that you had an obligation to those less enlightened than yourself. It was your duty to use any means necessary to raise them from their primitive state. If you were neither philanthropic nor especially troubled by moral scruples, you assumed you had the right to impose superior culture on all and sundry. To plunder the inferior was not exploitation, just the proper way for a superior species to conduct life. Philanthropic or not, there was general agreement that you had the right to bring them under your rule, and determine what was best for them (provided, of course, that that also served your own interests. . .).

Caught up in the buzz of imperial expansion, few Christians stopped to question the process very deeply, though it was committed believers who waded in to choke off the European involvement in the slave trade and protested to Parliament about some of the worst abuses of the poor and vulnerable at home and abroad. Here was a logical reformulation of Christendom: bring territory under the aegis of a "Christian" monarch, and expect people to be grateful for the good turn you had done them.

Except there was a twist in the tail. Not only were many conquered peoples not enthusiastic about embracing the confused amalgam of Christianity and humanism their imperial lords brought with them, the incoming powers of state and commerce weren't very convinced about it either. Whereas in the early centuries, imposing Christianity had been seen as a way of subduing and uniting peoples, now European soldiers and traders were more likely to see the introduction of the Christian faith as a destabilising action (bringing a backlash from outraged Muslim or Hindu devotees, for instance). It was certainly likely to curtail their own ambitions. There were definite economic and psychological advantages in keeping native peoples "poor and ignorant": it made exploitation easier to justify. In India, for example, the East India Company fought long and hard to keep missionaries out, though later when Queen Victoria became Empress of India she insisted that Christian missionaries should be given every assistance.

Whether or not you thought the native population (or, of course, the urban poor at home) was even capable of embracing superior Western civilisation depended on whether or not you considered those of a different skin colour as fully human. Or maybe you just thought God had ordained that some should be rich and powerful, and some should be poor and powerless, and to tinker with that was to fly in the face of God's will. We rightly find this way of thinking deeply offensive, but had we been alive and European then we might well have shared it.

It was into this very ambiguous context that the nineteenth century missionary movement was thrust. The greatest vigour sprang up among the evangelicals. This was to have profound implications, for these were men and women who simultaneously lived both within and without the framework of Christendom. Spiritual heirs of the Anabaptists and the Puritans, even if they remained members of territorial churches such as the Anglican church, they had already moved away in some important respects from the old assumptions. In particular, they looked for individual and highly personal faith, and believed that baptism and church attendance, in and of themselves, cut no ice with God. On the contrary, they said, God was looking for individual repentance and new birth. You could thus no more "make a community Christian" by force than fly in the air.

Evangelicals were to be found across denominational lines, but held a shared core of doctrine, practice and inherited influences. This was to be immensely significant, because they soon found it was easier to work together among themselves within the missionary enterprise than it was to work with those of their own denominations whose convictions were different. In due course, this led to the wave of interdenominational missionary societies which sprang up especially from the mid-nineteenth century onwards. This model remains widespread to this day.

Influenced by the Evangelical Revival in Britain and the Great Awakening in America, and later on by the Holiness movements of the nineteenth century, the focus was very strongly on the individual man or woman and on his or her state of grace. This was greatly reinforced by gatherings such as the Keswick Convention in the English Lake District, where devout Christians met year by year to seek a deeper spiritual life. This and similar conventions were to have a profound influence on many missionaries, encouraging a rather pietistic approach to faith, that is, concentrating on the believer's individual peace with God. In all these strands, the central doctrines were of Christ's person and work – and of course these lie at the very heart of the gospel. There was much less attention to the church and the corporate levels of Christian faith. Consequently, in large measure the inbuilt tensions between church and state in the Constantinian model could be mostly side-stepped and ignored, and they were.

In addition, and related to this, the evangelical missionary movement's origins and focus meant that "ordinary" lay people could do what needed to be done. For the first time for centuries, you did not have to be a priest or ordained to engage in meaningful ministry. You could be a carpenter, or a shoemaker, or a farmer – or even a housemaid. For, before long, women as well as men swelled the ranks of the missionary force, and by the 1860s outnumbered them. You might follow a trade to finance yourself and to give you a recognisable role in the host society, seeking to bear witness to Jesus Christ as you went about your daily business. Or you might be supported by friends back home so that you could devote all your time and energy to evangelism and discipling or translation of the Scriptures. Perhaps because these were ordinary men and women, by the middle of the century many other ordinary men and women believed they, too, could go to the ends of the earth, and the trickle became a growing torrent. And hundreds of thousands of Christian folk "back home" prayed and sewed and raised money. In the course of it, the need to reach the heathen became once more part of the church's daily conversation.

But there was a tragic and unforeseen downside, too. The study of theology and the practice of mission, which over many centuries had gradually drifted apart, now became decisively unhitched. With a few glorious exceptions, those who studied theology did not engage in reaching the unreached, and those who engaged in mission were too taken up with the enormity of their task to have much time or energy for being reflective. It is probably true to say that there were more missionaries who grappled with theological issues than theologians who grappled with mission issues. The very way in which theology had been done for centuries, shaped on the one hand by Christendom and on the other by a particular academic method, tended to make theology esoteric. All too little attention had been paid to exploring the frontier between doctrinal truth and the world of unbelief. The missionary, on the other hand, found himself continuously at that frontier, daily engaging with other religions, or the spirit world, not to mention cultural issues, that simply did not relate to anything in the traditional Western theological curriculum. Alexander Duff briefly tried to bridge that gap on his return to Scotland from India, but few listened.

As the nineteenth century rolled by, the British empire moved from triumphant strength to triumphant strength. Railways and steam ships and telegraph made travel and communications easier than ever before, with uncanny echoes of the first century. Mission schools spread the English language and literacy. Imperial armies enforced right of movement for Westerners. Trade boomed, as Africa and India and Asia were ransacked for cheap raw materials. Western philosophy, both Christian and humanist, seemed poised to rule the world. Islam and Hinduism appeared to have lost heart, and to be crumbling. In the first century, Palestine had been the crossroads between north and south, west and east; now, for a little while, Britain was the spider at the centre of the web of the world, with America not far behind.

No wonder many Christians felt God had sovereignly delivered the world into their hands, to conquer for Christ. One great effort, and the Great Commission would be completed, the world evangelised, and the Lord could return. That such a world church should be dominated by Europe and America was rarely questioned. Success, like power, can be very seductive. Was this faith or control? Was this love of God or confidence in human abilities? Maybe sometimes the dividing line between triumphalism and daring faith can be very hard to discern.

Artisans and aristocrats

William Carey, mending shoes in an obscure village outside London in the 1780s, and wondering how the church might reach the world for Christ, could scarcely have dreamed of what would happen in the next two hundred years. The modern missionary movement is generally reckoned to have begun with Carey, although that is perhaps rather simplistic, and there were already some Protestant societies in existence by then. However that may be, Carey's little booklet, the *Enquiry*, published in 1792 and establishing a powerful case for Christians' obligation to reach the heathen, came to be a famous landmark.

Carey was a pastor as well as a cobbler, and an extraordinary self-taught linguist and theologian. As he struggled to summarise the balance between divine sovereignty and human responsibility, he came up with the pithy slogan: "Expect great things from God; attempt great things for God". That could be inscribed across his life, as with a couple of companions he worked for forty years in north-east India. Like the Celtic missionaries, he set up a small community, and sent out well-trained local converts in pairs to pioneer elsewhere. Like the Jesuits, he saw the strategic importance of education and both taught in the government college in Calcutta and established Serampore College to train Indian Christians. Like Ricci, he respected local culture and learning, and became an expert in Indian horticulture and literature. Like the Reformers, he believed passionately that people needed to hear the word of

God in their own tongue, and he translated the whole or parts of the Bible into forty-four languages. Like the Puritans, he gave himself to preaching and prayer and writing. Yet, it seems he never sought especial recognition or reward, simply expected great things from God and attempted great things for God.

Carey never returned to England, but before his death an increasing number of Protestant missionary societies had come into being. Some were denominational, like the Church Missionary Society. Some focused on a very specific type of ministry, such as the Religious Tract Society, which produced vast quantities of very cheap literature explaining the Christian faith. Others were associated with a particular place of origin, such as the Berlin Missionary Society. Others again, such as the London Missionary Society, brought together people from different denominations. Yet more focused on a particular destination – or, daringly, took on the whole world.

It's hard to tell just why these new societies took on the form that they did. The simple answer is that like-minded people were naturally drawn together, and embarked on a common task. On the whole, denominational leadership was not very keen to put its full weight behind mission ventures, and wouldn't have known how to set about it if they had been. There was no obviously practicable means of getting complete denominational membership involved, but a small dedicated band of volunteers could get things moving. On the other hand, over the years some missions, perhaps rather grudgingly sanctioned in the first place by their denominational boards, did come in due time to involve large numbers of members, especially through the women's auxiliary groups set up to support missionaries. Often weekly, an amazing network of women – the lady of the Manor along with humble housewives, or perhaps a group of factory girls – would meet together to pray, to quilt or knit or sew, and to pour in their pennies. Together, they raised phenomenal sums of money.

Frequently a mission grew around an inspirational leader, or a personal friend, or a particular cause that drew people. At home, a committee would see to the channelling of finance and often give directions to those on the field. This sometimes led to bizarre and unworkable instructions, born out of ignorance and distance, and complicated by the length of time it took for letters to make their way back and forth across the world. At the field end, as numbers swelled, missionaries tended to gather together into small groups to give each other moral support and to staff the church, school and clinic which tended to complement each other. The resulting arrangement quite frequently looked remarkably like the monastic communities of the past, particularly where colleagues lived together on a mission compound.

If Carey was a trail blazer, a growing army marched close behind him. As numbers grew, and inspirational stories – often with a "shiver down the spine" element – trickled home, more people came forward to join them. Life expectancy was short; of course, it was not very long at home, either, but the unfamiliar diseases along with occasional martyrdom made it even shorter. Some perhaps were drawn by a spirit of adventure, which today might equally well express itself in very different ways. But, given the dangers and privations, by far the greater majority really were motivated by love for God and the desire to see people of every race and tongue come to faith in Jesus Christ. Extant letters, never written for the public eye, are often fragrant with love and faith and prayerfulness.

From the beginning, there was an extraordinary social mix. People who could not possibly associate with each other in towns and villages back home worked shoulder to shoulder overseas. That was a lovely reflection of the early church. Sometimes the social mix worked because in practice those who belonged to a missionary society nonetheless largely worked alone or with only one or two chosen companions. Many of those who became legendary were intensely individualistic, and while that sometimes made them rugged pioneers it did not always demonstrate in a heathen context the dynamics of Christian community life.

Among those who came from poor and unprivileged backgrounds are some of the best known names of all. David Livingstone, explorer of the mysteries of inland Africa, was a self-educated weaver. Mary Slessor, pioneer in Nigeria, was a factory girl. Gladys Aylward, who worked in both China and Taiwan, was a housemaid. Blacksmiths, shepherds, sailors and factory hands – every humble walk of life is represented in the records of mission societies. Even more remarkable are the men and women who emerged from the emancipated slave communities of the southern states of America, and who were taking their full place in mission overseas by the later part of the nineteenth century.

At first, it seemed that all that was needed was for a man or woman to have a lively personal faith and a strong sense of call, and limited education and lowly status was no handicap. But, as some of these early workers fell apart as they discovered that a love for God and a Bible did not by themselves equip them for survival in a totally alien environment, it became obvious that there must be a better way. Before long, training systems were set up back home to try to prepare new missionaries in advance. Later, the Bible College movement came to meet the needs of thousands of men and women in both North America and Europe, many of them brought to faith in Christ through evangelist DL Moody.

Often these converts were from the fringes of urban society, unskilled and with little or no formal education. Yet, as Moody's unconventional and compassionate preaching penetrated a mission field largely untouched by established denominations, it often produced deep new spiritual life. Further, these were men and women who had no doubt about the fact that they had needed to be saved from sin, and that others did, too. The training schools and Bible colleges alike concentrated on Bible knowledge, character formation and practical skills for ministry, and proved an effective pattern of discipling. They had more than a whiff of the monastery about them, and, like the best of the monasteries, turned out many dedicated workers. Thousands went overseas, while many others worked in the mission halls serving the urban poor who rarely felt at home in the mainstream churches.

But, along with the socially humble came a growing number of well-educated and even aristocratic volunteers. In the eighteenth century, some from "high society", such as the Countess of Huntingdon, had been deeply affected by Wesley and Whitefield's ministry, and had thrown themselves into the cause of the gospel. They brought not only wealth but also social influence – and the power to "get things done". At the turn of the nineteenth century, groups such as the Clapham Sect, of whom William Wilberforce is best known, and, a little later, individuals such as Lord Shaftesbury, all came from wealthy, privileged backgrounds and were passionately committed to mission at home and overseas. In America, some wealthy women, both married and single, were tireless and influential advocates for mission. Some, like Sarah Doremus, stayed within America. Others, such as Emma Whitemore, established rescue homes for street women all over the world.

By the last thirty years of the nineteenth century, the student world was also of key significance, and produced a steady stream of educated young men, along with some women, who joined missionary societies. As early as 1808 in America, a group of students in Massachusetts met regularly to pray for "the ends of the earth". In time, it was this group that was to spark off the earliest organised board in America for foreign missions, and in 1812 four couples and a single man, among them Adoniram and Ann Judson, set off for India and Burma. Students in a number of other denominationally linked colleges pressed their leaders to establish mission boards for them, too, and these were quite quickly formed. There was a pause during the Civil War, which tragically consumed people and resources, and equally tragically set Christian against Christian. But, in 1886, the Student Volunteer Movement was born, which drew together students from many different denominations. From it poured large numbers of graduates who believed there could be no higher calling than that of the foreign mission field.

Probably the students who had the most startling impact of all were the Cambridge Seven. This group of friends, all from wealthy and very privileged backgrounds, volunteered together to work in China under the auspices of the China Inland Mission. This had been formed in 1865 by James Hudson Taylor to take the Christian gospel throughout the interior of the vast mainland of China. It was a faith mission, which meant that there was no guaranteed wage, and no solicitation of funds. Members must look to God, presenting their needs to him through prayer, and trust in him alone to supply their needs. For the Cambridge Seven, educated at the most prestigious university in the world, accustomed to financial security, and with the natural prospect of very comfortable lives ahead, to risk everything to become missionaries, in a hostile environment at that, was deeply shocking to their social class. Yet, their dedication sent ripples far and wide, well beyond the shores of Britain. Crowds flocked to hear them speak wherever they went, the newspapers were full of them. Volunteers came forward in droves.

The China Inland Mission (CIM) broke new ground in a number of ways. Hudson Taylor insisted that the administrative heart of the mission must be in China, not in Europe or America. Decisions must be made within the cultural context and practical realities of those they were trying to reach, not be driven by the agenda and cultural assumptions of some far-off committees. This was probably possible because the CIM was interdenominational, and thus not tied to the directives of any one denomination whose centre was at that time almost inevitably in either Europe or America. It was an important separation of power from the West and some of the assumptions and constraints of Christendom, although "power" within the mission of course still rested with Westerners.

CIM missionaries were required to adopt Chinese dress, and wherever compatible with the gospel utilise Chinese cultural forms and way of life. Here were echoes of Ricci, long ago. The CIM was also the first Protestant missionary society to become robustly international, and also extensively to team up missionaries with native evangelists and Bible women. It was also the CIM that decisively ensured the role of women in the modern missionary movement. Probably because of Hudson Taylor's Methodist roots, he believed it to be scriptural for women to engage in every kind of ministry for which they were gifted, and among men as well as women and children. In the original party that sailed for China, he included seven single women along with the wives of married men. These were to be missionaries in their own right, not simply substitutes-at-hand when a wife died in childbirth, or maiden aunts to help care for a growing brood of children, or females to ensure the creature comforts of male missionaries. Soon, single women were pioneering, establishing churches and schools, travelling far and wide, while their married sisters also laboured in shared or complementary ministries alongside their husbands.

This was revolutionary in an era in which almost all denominations strictly limited what a woman was permitted to do in the churches back home. Just as once, ironically, some convents had spelt freedom for otherwise circumscribed women to serve God and community far beyond the domestic role, so now missionary societies flung wide doors of opportunity for many Christian women who dreamed of more satisfying lives. And they flooded through them. Thousands worked primarily with women and children, and in those many cultures where these were especially vulnerable and liable to exploitation the needs were enormous. Others worked freely among both men and women. By the close of the century, female missionaries far outnumbered male missionaries. From then till the present, that same pattern has remained unchanged.

Of course, there were those who disapproved. Some consigned missionary women to a kind of third sex, a different species who might do things ordinary women might not. Others decided that "natives" could be regarded as children, in which case it was permissible for women to teach and instruct them. Others simply shut their minds to what was happening. But, when many of these women came home on leave and shared stirring stories of what God was doing, told of privations and tears and triumphs, people flocked to hear them and listened enthralled. A spate of fine missionary books and hymns came from women's pens. Many of these highlighted the way in which African and Asian women were coming to faith in Christ and then becoming the most effective missionaries possible among their own people. Often that effectiveness flowed out of great weakness, for few women had either financial or social power.

The nineteenth century is a remarkable story of growth and vision. Under God, by the end of the century the church had become worldwide in a manner far different from anything seen before. By 1900, the missionary movement seemed unstoppable. Large numbers of Christians, in many countries, were deeply committed to the Great Commission, and understandably believed that very soon Christ's command could be fulfilled. Yet, in retrospect it is possible to see many things, especially in the uneasy link between mission and political power, and in the frequent failure to vest leadership in local believers, that were to cause great problems. Further, the growth had not gone uncontested. Not only had many missionaries laid down their lives through sickness or martyrdom, but also a swelling number of native Christians had also died for their faith. In some places, for example Japan and India, there had been terrible persecution interspersed with advance.

The twentieth century was to dawn with both sunshine and storms.

Questions

1. Why – apart from the sovereignty of God – do you think the nineteenth century became "the Great Century" for world mission?
2. How can we more effectively encourage men and women from every part of the social spectrum to become disciples and disciple-makers?
3. In every generation, Christians reflect some of the values and assumptions of their home cultures. What were the pluses and minuses of that in the nineteenth century missionary movement? What are some of the strengths and weaknesses of Western culture today as they affect our response to the Great Commission?
4. Why do you think women soon immensely outnumbered men in formal missionary work? What do you think were the consequences, good and bad, of that?

10

A New World Order

The twentieth century began with great optimism, but the church worldwide also suffered many grievous blows. Nonetheless, there was also amazing growth. By the close of the century, not only had the church come of age in many countries far beyond the traditional heartlands of Christian faith, but also nearly every country (though not yet every ethnic group) had at least a small group of local believers. And, by the end of the century, well over half of those professing Christian faith were in Latin America, Africa, and Asia.

A New World Order

Some want to live within the sound
Of Church or Chapel bell;
I want to run a rescue shop
Within a yard of hell.

CT Studd (1862–1931)

I am not worthy to follow in the steps of my Lord, but, like him, I want no home, no possessions. Like him I will belong to the road, sharing the suffering of my people, eating with those who will give me shelter, and telling all men of the love of God.

Sadhu Sundar Singh (1889–1929)

Christ sent me to preach the gospel and he will look after results.

Mary Slessor (1848–1915)

God walks "slowly" because he is love. If he is not love he would have gone much faster. Love has its speed. It is an inner speed. It is a spiritual speed . . . It goes on . . . at three miles an hour. It is the speed we walk and therefore it is the speed the love of God walks.

Kosuke Koyama

There is a net of love by which you can catch souls.

Mother Teresa (1910–1997)

With God anywhere, without him, not over the threshold.

John R Mott (1865–1955)

The church is the church only when it exists for others.

Dietrich Bonhoeffer (1906–1945)

Prayerfully, quietly, a little group of us sat together, facing a momentous decision. The country where we were was itself spiritually – and in every other way – very needy. Politically and economically, it was in turmoil. Yet, a cry for help had come from across the world, and we knew that one of our number had exactly the gifts and experience to meet that need. How could we spare her? We so badly needed her here! How could we possibly raise the money she would need? As it was, our colleagues lived barely at subsistence level. Yet, gently, tenderly, the Lord had brought conviction to her and to us all that she should go. And so, hesitantly and with nervous faith, we agreed she should be a love gift from the one country to the other, and that we would trust the Lord for all the consequences. It was costly for her, her family, and for us, her friends. But it marked the start of a stream of cross-cultural missionaries from that country, previously accustomed to being on the receiving end rather than the sending end. And what a blessing that has been to the church there!

The crumbling of empires

In the Western world, the nineteenth century drew to a close with a widespread sense of confident excitement. America had put the Civil War behind her, and was leaping from strength to strength. In Britain, Queen Victoria had been on the throne throughout most people's lifetime, giving a sense of continuity. And, since many European monarchies had intermarried, there was a general feeling that most disagreements were petty family squabbles. The Boer War in South Africa was an uneasy exception, with two Protestant powers at loggerheads.

The new century began with the Boxer Rebellion in China, in the course of which many missionaries and thousands upon thousands of Chinese Christians lost their lives. Here was a powerful sign from a proud and sophisticated ancient culture: Christianity was regarded as fundamentally Western, alien to China, and the tool of Western political and economic imperialism. Destroying the church was imperative if China was to regain her freedom from external control. The link between the Christian mission movement and expansionist empires, in place since Constantine, had become a terrible liability. This was despite the fact that in China, as in many other countries, the missionary force had been at the forefront of protest against some of the evils perpetrated against her by foreign powers, notably through the opium trade. Most Chinese could see only the apparent identification between church and Western powers, not the distinction between them.

Through the rest of the twentieth century, this same pattern was to be played out in country after country. In fact, it was often the countries where the response to the gospel had been greatest, or at the very least where the dissemination of Christian values through education had been widest, that sprang to oust the foreign powers. Ironically, it was often the Christian message that had made that inevitable, because it was this that had taught the dignity of human beings made in the image of God, regardless of colour or race. It was the Christian message that had encouraged people to look for change to redress wrongs. It was Christian schools that had brought education and literacy and exposure to Western ideas, including those of democracy, and that had given skills to nationals to undertake their own industrial projects, to train as nurses and doctors and teachers. And it was frequently missionaries who had given a sense of renewed pride in native languages, as they put them into writing, often for the first time, translated the Bible into those languages and then taught literacy so that converts could read it for themselves.

The Christian message, so long a captive to Christendom, had become profoundly subversive. By the middle of the century, almost all of the European empires had been dismantled. In Russia, the long-standing link between church and state had been destroyed by the Marxist Revolution of 1917. In Latin America, the process of shaking off imperial powers came earlier, mostly in the nineteenth century, but the Catholic Church often retained considerable political power. In Africa and Asia, most countries won their independence through war or negotiation by 1960. Where the former imperial power resisted granting independence, hostility to Christianity was often all the greater.

But it was the First World War that spelled the beginning of the end for the European empires, and that was also to have profound significance for the missionary movement. Four years before, in 1910, an international missionary conference had been convened in Edinburgh, Scotland. Attended by some 1,200 missionaries and church leaders, only seventeen were not Westerners, and very few were women, despite the fact that by then there were many hundreds of thousands of non-Western Christians, and that the majority of the missionary taskforce were women. One of their declared aims in coming together was to explore ways of establishing a unified world church, which at that time very few denominational church leaders were remotely interested in, but which seemed a pressing need in the context of Africa and Asia. In the event, they made little progress on that score, but the general message of the conference was one of incredible optimism. It was widely felt that the evangelisation of the world would soon be completed, that missionary reinforcements were not especially needed since the end of the task was in sight, and that Islam, Buddhism and Hinduism were all on the point of terminal collapse. The world was about to become truly Christian.

Nearly a century later, that all looks unbearably sad and naïve. Not only have Islam and Hinduism in particular experienced radical renewal through fundamentalist movements, there are still extensive parts of the world where the church hangs on by its fingernails if at all. And, far from becoming united, with a few minor but not insignificant exceptions, denominations all over the world have proliferated.

The passage from optimism and confidence to much greater

realism was swift and painful. The First World War immensely discredited the gospel in the eyes of men and women all over the world, as they saw so-called Christian nations slaughtering each other on a scale never witnessed before. For many Europeans, it was the justification of all their scepticism, and marked a decisive abandonment of the church by millions. For those looking on from further afield, it made all Christianity's claims to a nobler way of life seem utterly hollow. It swallowed up vast sums of money, destroyed the better part of a generation of young men, and shook European social orders to the core. All these had an enormous impact on the church in general, and on the missionary movement in particular.

Moreover, the evangelical wing of the church, which had been the most active of all in mission in the previous century, was now fighting grim battles of its own. From within, it was torn apart by disagreements over certain doctrines, for example the nature of the inspiration of Scripture, and eschatology (beliefs about the Lord's Second Coming and the end of time). From outside, it was increasingly being marginalised both by other sectors of the Church and also by a steadily more secular society. Society did not like it because it did not like its uncompromising message. The High Church did not like it because it did not, in their opinion, have a high enough regard for the church or for its sacraments. The liberal wing of the church, growing in size and confidence, did not like it because it considered evangelicals to be simplistic in their approach to the Bible. Liberalism had emerged largely out of the evolutionary theory which came into vogue in the nineteenth century, and from methods of criticism applied to the Bible and to ideas about religion.

So, in the aftermath of the First World War, the Western churches were in disarray, and attitudes to world mission once again deeply divided. Against all the odds, missionaries continued to pour out, but the gap between them and the churches back home widened. Sadly, as liberals distanced themselves from evangelism and concentrated on social action, evangelicals reacted by doing the opposite. This not only increased the polarisation between the wings of the church, but also led to long and bitter arguments among evangelicals. This was especially sad, because evangelical mission had a long history of caring for the poor, of meeting needs of mind and body as well as of soul, and of being an effective catalyst in social transformation. It was not till 1975 and the Lausanne Congress, more than fifty years later, that once again what came to be called wholistic mission, that is, mission to the whole person in the whole of his life, was widely accepted by evangelicals. Even after that, the arguments did not die down everywhere.

The Depression of the 1920s and 1930s, and then the Second World War, simply intensified the problems following the First World War. Yet, despite all that, the twentieth century also marked phenomenal growth for the church. There was an explosion of missions and missionary activity, and by the end of the century nearly every sizeable people group in the world had some viable Christian witness, although some smaller groups were as yet untouched. By the last quarter of the century, there was again in some quarters a growing confidence that by the year 2000 the Great Commission could be fulfilled everywhere.

There were a number of significant contributory factors to the explosion of growth, despite the problems. Firstly, early in the century, the Orthodox, Roman Catholic and Protestant streams of the Church were joined by another: the Pentecostal. This new movement, seeking to recapture the immediacy and power of the Holy Spirit for contemporary Christians, began in North America but almost simultaneously emerged in Wales and other parts of Europe. The enormous vigour of this movement was to have special impact on Latin America, where Pentecostalism is now the largest sector of the Church, and Africa. In both these continents, Pentecostalism speaks powerfully to cultures deeply affected by supernaturalism and animism, fits well with cultural exuberance, and more readily lends itself to cultural adaptation than do many Catholic and Protestant traditions.

Secondly, while earlier in the century there had been a growing multitude of national pastors and evangelists and Bible women, in the last few decades mission from the two-thirds world, that is, from the non-North American and non-European world, gathered pace at an incredible speed. By the beginning of the twenty-first century, it was computed that probably the majority of all missionaries worldwide were from Latin America, Africa and Asia. Many of these engaged in cross-cultural mission within their own national boundaries; for example, in India or Nigeria, where there are many different languages and cultures. In particular, Korea and Brazil produced large and dedicated missionary taskforces, who often had to overcome enormous barriers of language and finance to move to new countries. Oftentimes, these new waves of missionaries did not carry with them the baggage of being from imperialist nations; in fact, they often had themselves come from nations recently subject to another. This gave them acceptance where others could no longer go.

Thirdly, the latter part of the twentieth century saw the emergence of a large number of short-term missionaries. Mostly but not exclusively young people, these short-termers served cross-culturally for a few months or a few years, and then returned to their home countries to resume their careers. They frequently brought energy and idealism, and took home with them unforgettable life-changing experiences with which to nourish the next generation of obedience to world mission.

Fourthly, even under the difficult conditions of Communism, God had been doing marvellous things. In many parts of the former USSR (Russia and its satellite countries), the church grew quietly and surely, even in the face of persecution. There are many remarkable and beautiful stories of great faithfulness to Christ and of unbelievers coming to faith. In China, after terrible suffering during the Cultural Revolution, the church emerged with numbers multiplied. The true number of believers there is known only to God, but there is good evidence that in some regions many people are faithful, active disciples, quietly sharing the good news about Jesus in word and deed. It has been suggested that during the twentieth century the church had more martyrs than in all the previous centuries put together. We should be cautious about asserting that too confidently, because of course it is not possible to have absolutely reliable data. Nonetheless, it is clear that many, many Christian men and women died rather than turn their back on their Lord. As in the days of the early church, such faithful testimony has borne fruit beyond the wildest imaginings of persecutor and persecuted alike.

Fifthly, in country after country the church has come of age. Where missionaries failed to entrust leadership soon enough to national Christians, sometimes the Lord used political events or other means to wrest control away from those who would hang on to it. In many countries, missionaries now work alongside or under national leadership, bringing particular areas of expertise, or simply demonstrating the international nature of the people of God. With national leaders at the helm, it is often easier for believers to assume proper responsibility rather than looking to "rich foreigners". And, under national leadership, it is easier for the gospel to become less Western and more true to itself in another culture.

Sixthly, all over the world, men and women can hear God's word in their own tongue. Thousands of Bible translators have poured their lives into producing Scripture in local languages, so that today those languages where there are not yet complete Bibles are comparatively few, and those with no Scripture portions at all even fewer. This vital ministry has been helped by enormous strides in linguistics, understanding how languages work and how to make translations that are both accurate and colloquial. Then, through modern technology, it is more possible than ever before to make the fruit of all this labour available: cheaper mass printing, then radio, then videos, now even the internet, have all been pressed into service. Even in a remote tribal village, it may be possible to find people gathered around a solar-powered radio listening to Bible teaching in their own tongue. And in countries where Christianity is outlawed, by one means and another the message leaps over barriers.

Seventhly, the twentieth century became the great century of travel. The world's population is amazingly mobile. Occasionally, but increasingly rarely, you can find people who have never stirred further than a few miles from where they were born. It is very unusual indeed to find a complete community like that. Vast numbers of people leapfrog round the world on business or on holiday. On every continent, in every major city, there are economic migrants and political refugees. Stroll the streets of London or Sydney, New York or Singapore or Nairobi, and you find yourself surrounded by a blend of languages even more diverse than that on the streets of Jerusalem on that first Pentecost two thousand years ago. Citizens of countries even most hostile to the gospel rub shoulders with Christian men and women at airports, in university lecture rooms, in international gatherings for trade.

Lastly, in the years since the Edinburgh Conference in 1910, increasing attention has been given to issues of strategy, theology, and practice. How should we set about the task to be most effective? What exactly does God ask us to do? What does the church look like in different cultures? It is to these and related questions that we shall turn our attention in Part 3.

Gathering up the threads

We have caught only glimpses of the story, and many precious chapters have had to be left out. But perhaps it has been enough to make us realise how profoundly this is God's story, not ours. Even the most devoted and best-intentioned men and women have, with hindsight, frequently been guilty of the most appalling mistakes. Some have tried to impose Christianity by force. Others have been so frail and vulnerable that humanly speaking there could be no possibility of them ever achieving anything significant. Others again have been arrogant, or ignorant or simply stumbling in their grasp of the truth about Jesus. The forces arrayed against the church have often been overwhelming. At times it must have seemed as if the flame of faith must be snuffed out.

And yet, through it all, in fits and starts, the church has grown. In the mercy of God, there have always been those who have not only themselves been faithful disciples but who have also been fervent in enabling others to become disciples, too. Some compute that today about one third of the world's population would call themselves Christian, although that would include everything from highly committed to self-professedly nominal. This represents considerably more than any other religious bloc, including that of the Islamic world. About one quarter of the world is thought to be without any access at all to the Christian message, and the remainder is within reach of small but viable Christian communities.

We should rightly be cautious about how we use these kinds of statistics; at best they are well-informed guesses, and often extrapolated from necessarily partial-survey information. Nonetheless, they almost certainly show us something close to reality.

Which of those first disciples could have dared believe that one day somewhere approaching two billion people would profess to follow Jesus Christ? What an amazing work of God!

Questions

1. What factors and events of the twentieth century do you

think most helped, and which most hindered, the growth of the Christian faith?

2. If you could talk now to a first century disciple, which stories would you pick out to tell him? Why?

3. Much of Europe is now once again an urgently needy mission field. How might we set about "making disciples" there (including Britain!)?

4. At the beginning of the twenty-first century, what are the strengths and what are the weaknesses we have inherited from the twentieth?

PART III
Taking Stock

11

"Making Disciples" Revisited

"Making (or being) disciples" is not the same thing as simple numerical expansion of the visible church. In this chapter, we return to explore further some of the hallmarks of a true disciple.

"Making Disciples" Revisited

But, brothers . . . out of our intense longing we made every effort to see you . . . For what is our hope, our joy, or the crown in which we will glory in the presence of our Lord Jesus when he comes? Is it not you? Indeed, you are our glory and joy.

1 Thessalonians 2:17,19

True love is always costly.

Billy Graham

If we are willing to learn the meaning of real discipleship and actually to become disciples, the church in the West would be transformed, and the resultant impact on society would be staggering.

David Watson

All things are possible to him who believes; they are less difficult to him who hopes; they are more easy to him who loves, and still more easy to him who perseveres in the practice of these three virtues.

Brother Lawrence (1611–1691)

I sat in a gathering of church and mission leaders from all around the world. For several days we had talked and listened, laughed and wept, worshipped and interceded. Now, at the close, one after another shared what was deeply on their hearts. And, from Latin America, Africa and Asia came a common theme, repeated over and over in different words, a message to those of us from the West. "Go back and tell your people that we still need them," they said. "But please tell them this. We do not want your programmes, we do not want your money, we do not want those who only come to tell us what to do and how to do it. But, those who will come and stay long enough to learn our language and our ways, those who will come and learn to love us and stay long enough for us to learn to love them, those who do not think of us as a phase in their career but as brothers and sisters in God's family, those who will share our tears and our joys, our very lives: tell them, for these there will always be a welcome in Jesus' name."

In Part 2, we looked at some brief snapshots illustrating different ways in which the church grew from its tiny beginnings to today's worldwide phenomenon. Whether or not a particular group of Christians would articulate what they were doing in terms of the Great Commission, they all had this in common: they were committed to expansion.

This might be geographical or numerical or qualitative. It might be by enforcement or by persuading others voluntarily to join their numbers. It might be supported by all the machinery of state or be carried on doggedly in the teeth of fierce opposition and military power. It might be superficial or profound, for prestige or through martyrdom, protective of self-interest or crossing every frontier of race and class and religion out of love for God and for his world. It might be focused on the expansion of the church as institution, or it might be focused on individuals and their personal standing before God, or it might flow from a belief that "Christian civilisation" was superior to all others.

In all the muddle of motive and deed, from the very finest to the very worst, the only thing that makes sense of the contradictions of the story is the fact that the Lord himself gave his word that in spite of human fallenness he would and must build his church. Grace is stronger than anything, good or bad, that we can do. This is the shining continuous thread. Yet, inescapably, *expansion* and *making disciples* are not necessarily at all the same thing. It is clearly possible to expand the jurisdiction of the church as institution (and thus the number of people apparently associated with it) without a matching transformation of those same people into genuine disciples. Herding chickens into a sty doesn't turn them into pigs.

How these different groups set about expansion – and why – of course depended on their underlying beliefs about God, about their calling as Christians, about their relationship to those outside the Christian community. It depended on their goal: what did they want to achieve? It depended on their grasp (or lack of it) of God's ordained means for building his kingdom. It depended on their beliefs about baptism: does baptism sacramentally and automatically confer the status of disciple upon the recipient, or is baptism given to those already committed to be disciples, and, in the case of children, to those whose parents fully intend to raise them as disciples? And it depended on their context: they were often shaped by the assumptions and values of their generation and culture, though in some cases they were bravely counter-cultural. Of course, our analysis, looking back, may well be different from what they would have said about themselves in their own day. One day in the future there may well be a gap between the way we see ourselves today and the way future generations see us!

As we stand at the threshold of a new century, we do not start with a blank piece of paper. We inherit the legacies of previous generations, in particular those of the past century or so. In this section of the book, we shall try to understand some of these legacies, particularly as they relate to world mission and our understanding of the Great Commission. We will try to see how the recent past has shaped our present, both in terms of issues and also in terms of theory and practice.

But, before we do that, we need to return to the meaning of "making disciples", that command that is at the very heart of the Great Commission.

All you need is love

The Lord Jesus Christ famously summed up the core meaning of the Old Testament like this:

> "Love the Lord your God with all your heart and with all your soul and with all your mind." This is the first and greatest commandment. And the second is like it: "Love your neighbour as yourself." All the Law and the Prophets hang on these two commandments.
>
> *Matthew 22:37–40*

These deceptively simple words have caused Christian people a great deal of trouble. That is especially true in the modern West, where "love" has been widely devalued to mean heightened but fleeting feeling, or sexual attraction. The focus is on the emotional satisfaction of the one who "loves"; if a relationship is not emotionally rewarding and comforting, then "love" is not possible and the relationship should be discarded.

By complete contrast, the love of which Jesus speaks is far more than emotion, and moreover it is focused not on oneself but outwardly towards others. Here is love that is both active and reflective. It involves the commitment of one's total personality. It demands action, challenges attitudes and values, and stretches the mind. It is both passionate and deliberate, it engages the senses and expands our creativity. Every part of being human – of being made in the image of God – is caught up in this love. Because of the sheer diversity of human beings, we should not look for uniformity, but we should be able to see recognisable hallmarks of divine character. Totalitarian love for God is to be linked inseparably to love for those around us. And it is this combination, of love for God and love for others, that makes us into disciple-makers, "doers" of the Great Commission.

It is not love without boundaries. Extravagant it may be, but nonetheless love itself is defined by God, and outside those definitions we may have sentiment or good intentions or strong emotion, but not what God calls love. Because love is one of the names of God, love must mirror his character and nature to be love. So, it is bound up with truth and purity and righteousness. Further, it is not abstract. It is only possible in the context of personhood and relationship. God is love because of the perfection of committed relationship between the Persons of the Trinity. Christians are called to mirror that, even though the reflection may be rather shadowy in the here and now.

If we seek to make disciples without this love, we may become strategists (treating people as statistics or impersonal digits), or controllers (they must fit into our declared objectives), or power addicts (enjoying the buzz of bending others to conform to what we determine). On the other hand, without divinely informed love, perhaps we will condone what is not acceptable to God (for example, the syncretism in a person who wishes to become a disciple of Jesus Christ without letting go of other gods). This is not the way in which to bring people to be disciples of Jesus Christ, fellow-learners on a journey of pilgrimage. To make disciples requires us to share our lives with others, to respect them, to enter into their hurts and fears and hopes and dreams, to listen and admit that we do not know all the answers, to be willing to suffer for them. And all that, with great humility, must be within the boundaries of God's truth. Love relationships demand no less.

Discipleship and disciples

The Great Commission does not tell us to teach discipleship. It tells us to make disciples.

At first glance, that may seem like a classic case of splitting hairs. But behind it is a very important truth. "Discipleship" is abstract, "disciple" is personal. You can design a course on discipleship, with or without getting involved with any of the people for whom it is designed. But you can only make disciples by engaging life to life, person to person. That's why the Lord Jesus walked and talked, ate and prayed, laughed and wept with his disciples, instead of arranging for them to be sent a manual. He made disciples by sharing his life with them.

It is easy to lose sight of the fundamental importance of this. We cannot ourselves be disciples of the Lord Jesus Christ until we have a life-sharing relationship with him, however embryonic that relationship as yet may be. We cannot make disciples until we have a life-sharing relationship with other people. Great Commission people must both be disciples themselves, in a life-sharing, learning relationship with God; and also be prepared to commit themselves to meaningful long-term life-sharing relationships with others. Making disciples is not primarily a task so much as the forging of organic relationships which lead to mutual growth and progressive transformation.

Sadly, too much twentieth century discussion was about "doing the job", or persuading others "to make a decision for Christ", and too little about deepening love for the King – about the meaning of being a disciple for life. The explosion of technology and of mass media has seduced many Christians into thinking that mass impersonal influence "does the job", and that vast resources should be poured into these. While the supportive (and helpful) role of much mass media is beyond doubt, the fact remains that few people come to faith, and fewer still persevere in the life of the disciple, without authentic friendship with other believers. Real relationships, and shared love for the Lord, remain crucial to making disciples.

Jesus' call to his disciples is a call to embark on a journey, a pilgrimage, lasting all the rest of our lives. We know our destination – to come to where the King lives in glorious splendour – but we do not know all the details of the way. We do not know all the details of the way because we have not been this way before, and we have not yet arrived at the destination. This is a journey of faith, of new beginnings every day, in committed relationship with the invisible but ever-present God, and in the company of an extraordinarily diverse group of fellow-travellers. It is a journey of faith where we trust that the map that is given us is accurate because the One who has given it is trustworthy – he does not deceive us – and he has passed this way before. It is a journey of faith because the unseen, says God, is more real than the seen, even though the seen may seem often to contradict what God declares to be the real truth. The disciple of Jesus Christ must often live in ways which are puzzling or downright unintelligible to unbelievers.

But, the disciple does not travel alone, or even only in the company of God. He travels in a great crowd of fellow-travellers, past and present, seen and unseen, near and far. The disciple community has the opportunity to demonstrate communal life of a different order, where self-centredness gives way to loving service of others, violence to peace, alienation to reconciliation, greed to generosity, darkness to light. The transforming impact of the Spirit at work in God's people is to produce a visual aid that gives credibility to the accompanying explanation: "God saves! We're going to see the King!"

Moreover, this communal life, pointing as it does to the God who makes it possible, is always to be a dramatic challenge to the surrounding world. It is in juxtaposition that light and darkness are seen to be what they truly are. The challenge is both one of condemnation of the darkness, and also a glorious invitation to join the disciple community and set out to meet the King.

Any part of this disciple community may be rich or poor, educated or ignorant, young or old, international or tribal. The point is that in its context, in the place where it is living out its pilgrim life, it must stand out as different from its surroundings in embodying righteousness – displaying the character of the King – and point to the reality of the rule of God, present and future. At the same time it is self-confessedly a learning community, a community still being shaped and formed and transformed, even while it travels.

What a standard for Great Commission people! Yet this is the fundamental calling of the church, wherever it is found. As you go, wherever you go, make disciples, embraced on the one hand by the Lord's authority and on the other by the Holy Spirit's presence.

Against this background, let us return to taking stock of where we are at the beginning of the twenty-first century. We will approach this through looking in turn at some theological issues, some issues of context, and some issues of strategy.

Questions

1. In the community where you live, what kind of profile do Christians have? Are they known as "the people who cause parking problems on Sundays"? "That odd lot up the road in the old fortress of a building – don't know what they do"? "Friendly, helpful. . ."? "The ones who show us how to know God"? What might you need to do to demonstrate you are a community of disciples who love to see others also become disciples?
2. In today's very materialistic world, how can Christians help one another to keep our eyes on our final destination?
3. In some parts of the world, there are many people who consider themselves to be Christians (as opposed to being Muslims, or Hindus, or atheists, or. . .) but who show few of the signs of real discipleship. How might we address the problems of nominal Christianity?
4. In your local church or fellowship, what are the things that hinder you from loving one another in the way Christ calls

us to? What are the things that prevent us from having our
lives deeply bound up with one another as fellow-disciples
and pilgrims? What changes could make a significant
difference?

12
Danger! Theologians at Work!

Theological reflection and practical action should be inseparable. But, often that has not been the case, and our grasp of discipleship, and of disciple-making, has been distorted as a result. In this chapter, we look at the relationship between reflection and practice, and consider some areas where the church worldwide faces particular challenges.

Danger! Theologians at Work!

Most of us [who write theology] do not listen as we write.

Choan-Seng Song

In a continent that proclaimed itself "Christian" since the sixteenth century there has been a need to come to terms with a form of mission that reduced the gospel to a minimum in order to keep within the fold the maximum number of people. . . "As a result the church, far from being a factor for the transformation of society, becomes merely another reflection of society and, what is worse, another instrument that society uses to condition people to its materialistic values" [Padilla].

Samuel Escobar

. . . Overcoming violence and building peace is an indispensable part of Christian mission.

Andrew Kirk

The ethnocentricism of a large part of the missionary enterprise not only prevented sufficient understanding of African religious tradition, but also led to a theological misapprehension of the nature of the Christian gospel itself.

Kwame Bediako

Some of God's promises are written in invisible ink, only in the flame of suffering do they become visible.

Wang Ming-dao

Western Christians have failed . . . to declare God's perspective on the plight of our billion hungry neighbours.

Ronald Sider

When first we went to Asia, we found ourselves in the midst of political turmoil, and surrounded by many different realities, social and spiritual, that we had not encountered before. It quickly dawned on us that our friends were facing issues that simply did not get addressed in the traditional Western theological curriculum. It wasn't that that framework wasn't valuable any more – it was – but It so clearly wasn't the whole story. So, we were constantly scurrying back to the Bible with questions we hadn't asked before, and wouldn't have known how to answer had they been asked us. It was marvellously faith-stretching! Our friends would keep saying to us, "Is that British or biblical? Because, if it's British we don't want it, but if it's in the Bible, show us, and we want to obey." And the glorious thing was that though we hadn't noticed those things before, because we hadn't been looking for them, we found God had so much to say to these new questions. We learned so much more about his love and all-sufficiency.

Theology and theologians tend to have a very bad press in much of the Christian community. This is paradoxically both entirely understandable and entirely incomprehensible. Either way, it has had some tragic consequences. It is entirely incomprehensible because theology is literally the study of God, and this of all things should be the delight and glad preoccupation of his people. Growing in the knowledge and love of him should be the integrating purpose of our days. But, it is also entirely understandable. Theologians themselves have all too often discredited not only themselves but also their labours by the way in which they have set about things, the irrelevance of what they have majored on, and the hi-jacking of theology out of the reach of the ordinary believer. And, in passing, a surprising and tragic proportion of twentieth century Western theology had very little to say about God that was even remotely recognisable as the God and Father of our Lord Jesus Christ.

The worldwide church encompasses an amazing diversity of

temperaments, cultures and traditions. Among them, the "stirrers and shakers" have often been very activist: the main thing that matters is doing things. Others, including most of the theologians, have been primarily reflective: the main thing that matters is thinking about things. In the previous chapter, we thought about the way the Lord calls us to love him with our whole being. Doers need to be thinkers, and thinkers need to be doers!

Of course, there have been plenty of Christian men and women who have been marvellous exceptions, and have been both activist and reflective, but by and large the generalisation holds true. So, rather few theologians in the history of the church have been activists at the cutting edge of the church where faith meets unbelief; and rather few activists at the cutting edge of the church have been reflective theologians. Ever since Constantine, theologians have tended to work within the Christian community and focus their efforts on talking to those already "inside". This has dulled the engagement of theological discourse with the unbelieving world. It has separated mission and theology. It has domesticated theology and marginalised mission. It has been left to mission activists to engage with the unbeliever, and the resultant theological exploration has rarely made its way back into traditional theological textbooks and curricula.

From as early as the second century onwards, the most influential theologians were usually philosophers or lawyers before they became theologians. That shaped the way they "did theology", and established patterns which were not entirely helpful. From the fourth century on, the Western church almost exclusively couched its theology in the form of linear classical argument, and, with many permutations, that remains the dominant approach to theology to the present day.

As the church has spread beyond the Western world, especially in the past century, this theological heritage has been something of a liability, in at least three distinct ways.

Firstly, missionary pioneers are activists. Consequently, many of those who laid the foundations for the church in new areas in the nineteenth and twentieth centuries had limited theological acuteness. They were (rightly) keen to "save the heathen out of darkness" but may have had a rather narrow biblical and theological repertoire as they sought to disciple their converts. Considerable stretches of Scripture, and many vital areas of theology, were often set on one side as "too complicated for these simple people". This is always a dangerous route to travel. It is not only patronising and inaccurate in its assumptions about the potential spiritual maturity of those different from ourselves. It is also that the whole people of God need the whole of God's revelation. We will return later to some consequences of this selectivity. It is salutary to note that this was especially a problem among some (but not all) evangelicals: "What matters is the simple gospel!" they might say. These tended to take theological reflection and theological education less seriously than did, say, non-evangelical Protestants or Roman Catholics (whether or not what these latter groups exported was what was appropriate). Evangelicals are still trying to catch up lost ground in some places in Asia and Africa.

Secondly, traditional Western theology had rather little to say to the most pressing issues facing many missionaries and infant churches. This was one reason why some missionaries were impatient with it. There might be passing reference to other religions, but there was little attempt to interact with them at a deep level. After all, few Western theologians encountered other world religions, with the possible exception of Judaism. Is there any salvageable truth about God in Islam or Hinduism or Buddhism? If there is, how should one build on it? If there is not, how should one teach about the true and living God? There was little help in the face of endemic spirit practices, or ancestor practices. How does God relate to the spirit world? How should Christians relate to it? Is polygamy a cultural social arrangement or a defiance of a creation ordinance? Were all the generations of ancestors who lived and died before the first bearers of the Good News about Jesus arrived irretrievably lost? Any or all of these might be far more pressing concerns than the niceties of how much water makes a baptism valid, or whether every congregation must have both deacons and elders, or convoluted discussions as to how exactly human and divine came together in the Lord Jesus Christ. Consequently, on the one hand some very important areas of traditional theology were neglected (and the result of that may be seen today in breakaway cults, or churches with some very odd beliefs). And on the other hand, pressing issues – because unfamiliar – were not always recognised by Westerners as the legitimate subject of theological reflection. They thus were often dealt with pragmatically rather than in relation to revelation about the being and character of God.

Thirdly, the problem was not only with the *content* of theological reflection but also with the *method*. While Europe and the Protestant world tend to have been dominated by linear patterns of thinking and arguing, with a high value placed on logic and reason, in other parts of the world other patterns prevail. Many cultures transmit beliefs and tradition from one generation to the next primarily through storytelling, which may be roughly linear but is narrative (with lots of loose ends) rather than building a logical case. Some storytelling to Western ears is not linear at all: there is no beginning-middle-ending, only apparently random bits strung together. Some cultures transmit their most important beliefs through parables or proverbs. Some cultures explore ideas through spirals – "going round in circles". Some cultures integrate reflection and sensory experience much more closely than Western theologians are familiar (or comfortable) with.

The intriguing thing is that in fact all of these patterns can be found in Scripture, as God communicates truth to his people through narrative and history, poetry and parable, vision and law, reasoned argument and powerful emotion. All these and more are pressed into service to reveal truth about God. But, the traditional style of "doing theology" in Western circles is much more restricted. This not only exported restricted models to the non-Western world, it also made Western theologians slow to recognise the validity of theological reflection bubbling up in unfamiliar forms. The consequence has been mutual impoverishment. Today, some parts of the non-Western church would be considerably helped by attention to tried and tested areas of traditional theology. Equally, Western churches urgently need help from non-Western churches as much of the West becomes once again a pioneer mission field. This mutual exchange could contribute powerfully to the dismantling of the unbiblical notion that mission is "from the West to the rest".

It is not being implied that there has been deliberate or malicious intent in any of the above. On the contrary, probably a very high proportion of the church's theologians on the one hand and mission trail-blazers on the other have been men and women of high integrity, seeking to serve their Lord and Master. It is simply that for all of us there is a very powerful tendency to assume that the familiar is normative and anything else an aberration. Nor do we easily grasp our own blind spots. Let us look briefly at three areas which illustrate this, which have had an important impact on the spread of the church worldwide in recent decades.

The church and the churches

The last thirty years of the nineteenth century saw a great swell of men and women eagerly setting out to the far corners of the world in obedience to the Great Commission. Many of them had come to faith themselves, or sensed a call to become missionaries, through evangelistic campaigns, revival meetings, and conventions conducted alongside – and outside – the mainstream denominations. They might become, or even already be, members of those denominations, but nonetheless their own significant spiritual milestones might very well be established outside them. A growing number of mission agencies drew members from across the denominations. Their unifying bond was not shared churchmanship (in the sense of all coming from the same denomination) but shared commitment to a personal Saviour, and a rather individualistic view of salvation.

Inevitably, in those early years the majority of them went to places where there was as yet no established church, or where it was at best very young and new. Alone or with a handful of colleagues, they set out to pluck individual souls from the clutches of Satan, and then to band them together into little congregations. If you came from a denominational mission, of course you were expected to create a replica and outpost of your denomination back home, and the problem of what kind of church should take shape, and how it should be organised, was neatly taken out of your hands. But for the far greater majority, each new congregation was rather self-contained and how it developed might depend quite heavily on the particular idiosyncrasies of the founding missionary. As the years rolled by, and other missions came to the same geographical area and also planted churches, the growing headache of Western multiple denominations was simply exported and repeated.

The twentieth century Church Unity movement, through the World Council of Churches and other initiatives, was one response to this situation. It was a genuine attempt to search for ways by which different branches of the Christian church could relate to one another rather than ignore (or compete against) each other. The initial impetus came from observing the obscenity of confusing fragmentation in parts of the world where Christian witness was (probably) young, certainly fragile, and hindered by the internecine squabbles between different sectors of the church. Of course, the problem was that because different traditions of the church had evolved differently, and had some significantly different beliefs and practices, the only way to bring them together in any structural way generally involved being deliberately vague or ambiguous theologically. While the movement undoubtedly fostered civilised conversation between some sectors of the church, and even led to a few mergers, it did not achieve its avowed goal of creating one united universal church structure. And, whatever the strengths and weaknesses of the unity movement, the twentieth century was marked by an ever-accelerating proliferation of new denominations.

In sharp contrast with the unity movement, some have argued that the church grows best where little cell groups of believers, free from all external restraints or denominational links, simply grow in their own way and independently. In due course, some of their members may go to a new district or community and start all over again, but they, too, should have complete independence to grow in their own way. They do not need to relate to any other part of the Body of Christ. Others argue that unity matters, but it is spiritual and organic, not structural or visible, and local churches will relate naturally to those similar to themselves, and not to those that are different. Others argue that God anoints some individuals as inspiring leaders, and churches grow best around them. These leaders may be "apostles" or "prophets", and may claim special revelation from God for those they lead. Some claim that the church for centuries has been so decadent and misled (and misleading) that God can no longer use any part of it, but is starting all over again with a new generation of churches which will, for the first time since Pentecost, get things right.

So, today, we are left with some large, troubling, and seemingly intractable problems. How should one part of the church relate to other parts? What kind of over-arching corporate identity should Christians have? What boundaries of diversity can there be while still being authentically "Christian church"? Is what unites us in the face of an unbelieving world more important and fundamental than the things that divide us? It is easy to have *simple* answers, but these are often *simplistic* and *inadequate*. It is also easy to wash our hands of the questions, and say that there is too much urgent work to do: let's focus on the task of seeing people saved. But that, too, won't do. For one thing, it once again creates a divergence between thinking and doing, in disobedience to the Lord's command. For another, it is precisely because of the communal dimension of "making disciples" that we cannot ignore issues about the nature of the church, and the relationship between different parts of the Body of Christ. Great Commission people must be Church people. We still have a long journey ahead of us in resolving these questions. Until we do, God's people in different parts of the world will be hampered in responding in a coherent way to Christ's mandate. And, until we do, we shall not readily recognise what God is doing in pilgrim-companies different from our own.

Re-enter left: the Holy Spirit

Of course, the Holy Spirit has never been absent. Had he been, there could not have been dynamic Christian life, and clearly (in God's mercy) there have been many evidences of authentic spiritual vitality all down the centuries. The Lord had given his word: "surely I am with you always, to the very end of the age". And, always, God keeps his word.

Nonetheless, Western Christianity from the eighteenth century onwards was frequently rationalistic, and did not know how to relate to God as supernatural Being. The supernatural was the province of magic and superstition. It was right for the church to want to dispose of magic and superstition, but not right that a sense of the mystery of God, and awareness of him as supernatural – that is, literally, beyond natural – should also be discarded. At the same time, during the nineteenth century especially, there was in some circles a great hunger for a deeper experience of holiness, and also a longing for revival. The latter was often thought of as a special, sovereign visitation of God, which would produce a deep and widespread conviction of sin, a gathering of many unbelievers into the church, and visible manifestations of God's presence, such as there had been at the very beginning.

Perhaps in gracious answer to many prayers, perhaps as a dramatic corrective to the pride in human progress which was subverting much of the church, perhaps for reasons we shall never know this side of Glory, at the start of the twentieth century the Pentecostal movement burst on to the scene. At first it was regarded with suspicion by most sectors of the church. It seemed dangerous, emotion-charged, irrational – all things which were assumed by many to belong to an earlier evolutionary stage, from which the church had now progressed. But, in particular, the Pentecostals gave a very high profile to the current activity of the Holy Spirit, evidenced by gifts such as tongue-speaking or prophecy or healing. To Catholics, this seemed to undermine the sacraments (which they believed to be the chief channel of the Spirit); to most Protestants, it seemed to undermine the place (and sufficiency) of the Bible (which the Reformers had believed to be the chief channel of the Spirit).

For some time, traditional Western theological attention to the Holy Spirit had been rather scant. By contrast, nineteenth century missionary literature (letters, journals, books) has much more to say about him, and certainly much more to say about the reality of the supernatural altogether. This was perhaps inevitable as they encountered the demonic in unfamiliar forms, and tried to work out how to respond, and as they repeatedly found themselves in situations where they knew that only God himself at work in power could change the minds and hearts of the people around them. Here was theology at the cutting edge once again.

Nonetheless, the missionary community did not generally

embrace Pentecostalism – the theological gap was often too wide – and Pentecostalism swiftly subdivided into many different denominations. But, separate though it was, this stream soon impacted the wider church beyond its own immediate boundaries: it made theological debate about the Holy Spirit in the contemporary church inevitable, and it heightened expectations that God could still do extraordinary and supernatural things to authenticate his church. It polarised Christians between those who believed the gifts of the Spirit should all be available to God's church for all time, and those who believed that many of the gifts of the Spirit (especially some of those at the heart of Pentecostal claims and experience) were given for the original apostolic age only. It stimulated thinking about *how* the Holy Spirit brings life through the study and preaching of the Bible today. Further, it paved the way for the Charismatic Movement, which emerged in the middle of the twentieth century, and which was to modify significantly mainstream denominations as well as itself produce many new denominations.

Pentecostalism, and later the Charismatic Movement, very quickly spread in certain parts of the world. For example, there seems a special cultural affinity with much of Latin America, and with sub-Saharan Africa (and African communities in North America and Europe). Perhaps there are temperamental and sociological affinities. Certainly, where Christianity tended to be overlaid over a strong residual animism, Pentecostal emphases powerfully resonated with the felt needs of the people, both inside and outside the church. There were natural role connections: for instance the prophet could replace the soothsayer, the healer the witchdoctor, the apostle the tribal leader. Moreover, these replacement roles were especially attractive where traditional communities were being broken up through urbanisation.

Further, both Pentecostalism and later the charismatic churches gave far more scope for expressing worship through dance and new forms of music. Dramatic events (healings, tongue-speaking, etc) brought immediacy and direct involvement – a sense of touching the power of God for oneself. This often contrasted sharply with traditional Catholic worship, which, to be sure, had aesthetic power, but tended to be acted out from the front, with most people as spectators. It contrasted, too, with traditional Protestant approaches which often seemed to offer information for the mind but perhaps little for the rest of the human personality.

On the one hand, the Pentecostal and charismatic churches have grown exponentially in the past fifty years, and some observers conclude that it will be these groupings that will be most significant in church growth in the future. In particular, the Pentecostal churches have been more effective than most in making disciples among the urban poor, the marginalised, and the poorly educated. Since, worldwide, this is where population explosion tends to be happening, this is clearly of enormous significance. The charismatic churches have been more effective at reaching middle-class socio-economic groups worldwide, and this group is growing, and growing in influence, in many countries.

On the other hand, a troublingly large number of sects and sub-Christian groups have spun off out of either Pentecostal or charismatic roots. In reacting against former over-rationalisation of the faith, Pentecostal and charismatic churches may be especially vulnerable to being led away from non-negotiable Christian essentials, and may be too ready to regard spiritual experience as self-authenticating. Leaders who claim to be apostles or prophets may be hard to challenge, and can too easily lead others astray, or become cult leaders rather than servant-leaders of Jesus Christ.

The Lord urged us to love him with mind and heart and whole personality, and to teach obedience to *all* his commandments. Church history shows how hard this apparently is, and how readily we are all selective. Yet, without a doubt, all over the world there are fine disciples whose lives show the loveliness of Jesus Christ and who are part of the great Pentecostal and charismatic streams of today's church. For this we should praise God. Further, these streams in turn have brought intriguing change into many sectors of the Roman Catholic (at least at the grass roots level, for example in Latin America and the Philippines) and into many parts of the Protestant churches. This has changed alignments and groupings of some denominations, and also made it possible in a way not dreamed of a century ago for believers from different traditions on occasion to experience spiritual fellowship together. This in turn has made many younger Christians impatient of historic divisions in the church. On the one hand, this may produce a far more effective sense of unity than the World Council of Churches achieved. On the other, theology, and earnest commitment to try to be faithful to God's word and eternal truths, may once again be set aside (as they should not be) in pursuit of shared experience.

Cry freedom!

If Latin America has been one of the places where Pentecostalism has made its most dramatic strides, it is also the place where an electrifying new movement developed within the Roman Catholic Church. Liberation Theology was partly a reaction to the issue raised at the beginning of this chapter – the insulation of theological study from the real context of daily life for most Christians, and certainly from the point at which they collided with the unbelieving world. Traditional theology at the time simply did not have anything much to say to issues of oppression, injustice and grinding poverty, as experienced by a very large part of the population. The situation was made all the worse because the church was itself a wealthy landowner, and also because it supported the very vested interests which kept the masses in such appalling conditions.

One of the gravest problems with the Constantinian model of church–state relations (as obtained in most Latin American countries) is that the church ceases to be prophetic.

Of course, it is not that the Bible has nothing to say about poverty and injustice and oppression. On the contrary, the Bible has a great deal to say about them, and the Lord Jesus himself on various occasions couched his own mission in terms of bringing good news to the poor, and deliverance for the oppressed. But the church was remarkably silent about that. If anything, the teaching was that the poor were poor by God's sovereign choosing and must be faithful in their poverty without complaint. Had the church been "Good News" for the poor, as it should have been, and concerned with Christian righteousness for the whole of life for the whole of society, the story might have been very different.

But then, a little group of young Roman Catholic theologians dared to challenge the church. Excited by Marxist social analysis, they concluded that there could be no justice without a radical redistribution of resources and a complete reorganisation of social structures. Like Marx, they tended (wrongly) to regard the poor as righteous by virtue of being poor, and the wealthy as wicked simply because they were rich. And, like Marx, they taught that theory (in this case, theology) must be evaluated *and formulated* from the starting point of the concrete realities of the people's situations, rather than evaluating life in the light of the theory.

But, unlike Marx, they believed that the church could become the instrument of reform and renewal if only it recognised that God had "a preferential option for the poor". Using the story of the Exodus, they saw salvation in terms of rescue from exploitation by those with power: God intended his people to be delivered from injustice, and to come into a life of freedom and plenty. In fact, the New Testament does not draw a parallel between Exodus and salvation, but between Passover and salvation, and that distinction is very important when we look at Liberation Theology. But, despite that, no-one could deny the explosive effect of their teaching. The church authorities tried in vain to contain the impact, but in no time numerous priests and laity were enthusiastically following the new teaching. They were not trying to implement Communist regimes, but they were trying to bring about radical change to both church and state.

Like most renewal movements, this one has been messy, with some events and ideas which do no credit whatsoever to the cause of the gospel. In some cases, for example, both in Latin America and later in Africa, it has been used to justify violence and brutality – even murder – against those with land or property, and the forcible seizing of businesses. In some cases, the end product has unquestionably been Marxism masquerading under a church veneer. At the same time, Liberation Theology has also led to multitudes of lay people taking direct responsibility for the way they live their daily lives as Christians, seeking patiently to engage in social transformation as well as personal devotion. It has brought a far deeper consciousness of what it means to be disciples of Jesus Christ. Countless small groups have sprung up where Christians meet to study the Bible for themselves to try to discover what God has to say about righteous living: what it looks like, how to set about it. These "base ecclesial communities" have been the locus of much earnest discipling.

Some Protestants also quickly adopted Liberation Theology, Marxist social analysis and all. This was particularly easy in some parts of the liberal churches. But, in Latin America, a group of young evangelical leaders also struggled with issues of justice and oppression and gross poverty, and why these things should be so prevalent in a continent with a long Christian history. As they sought to use the Bible as the basis of their social analysis, they concluded that the gospel does indeed have immense social dimensions, that issues of justice and transformation are rightly the concern of God's people because they are concerns of God's heart. In due course, these men and others from other parts of the world became the catalysts for immense changes in the way most evangelicals the world over approach these issues, in both theology and in practice.

Poverty and injustice are still tragically the daily experience of countless millions. But, all round the world, God's people are seeking to bring change, to speak out on behalf of the voiceless, or to enable them to have a voice themselves. Great Commission people have recovered a vital part of the Lord's teaching. All the same, if the gospel is to have credibility in the twenty-first century, the church will surely have to speak more bravely, and act more sacrificially, on behalf of the world's poor. At the same time, there are many shining examples of transformed and transforming Christian communities to be found among the poor and oppressed, in the shanties of Rio de Janeiro or among the rubbish tips of Manila, hanging on doggedly in the ghettos of New York, or living in the violence of some South African township. Here is discipleship at the frontiers.

The church. The Spirit. Poverty and injustice. These are just three issues among many where it seems that the amazing growth of the church during the twentieth century has brought theological challenges we dare not ignore. In the light of these things, how then shall we "love the Lord [our] God with all [y]our heart . . . and soul . . . and mind"? Truly, we are disciples on a journey of discovery!

Questions

1. How would you explain what the church is supposed to be to a friend with no prior experience of it but now beginning to be drawn to the Person of Jesus Christ?
2. Besides those suggested above, what other theological challenges do you think may be facing the church

worldwide today? What has been *neglected* to lead to the current situation? What challenges have arisen because of changes in external circumstances?

3. How can you personally, and your local church or fellowship, integrate reflection and action more closely?

4. In the community where you live, what are some of the issues of injustice affecting people inside and outside the churches that Christians should speak out about? How might you bring about change?

13

Liverpool isn't Lagos isn't Lahore

Is the gospel always the same wherever and whenever it is proclaimed and lived out? Yes – and no! While there are fundamental truths that can never change, how they are communicated, and how authentic discipleship is lived out, will vary from setting to setting. So, how can the Christian message, and Christian communities, be "incarnated" in each context so that they do not obscure the truth but rather display it openly and truly?

Liverpool isn't Lagos isn't Lahore

Let us in everything unsinful become Chinese, that by all means we may save some. Let us adopt their costume, acquire their language, study to imitate their habits . . . live in their houses.

James Hudson Taylor (1832–1905)

The church enters a danger zone when it is no longer self-consciously critical of its relation to culture and is no longer asking what is the path of faithful discipleship. The church must always adapt to its culture in such a way that it communicates the gospel credibly.

Wilbert Shenk

That Word is to pass into all those distinctive ways of thought, those networks of kinship, those special ways of doing things, that give the nation its commonality, its coherence, its identity. It has to travel through the shared mental and moral processes of a community, the way that decisions are made in that community. Christ is to become actualised – to become flesh, as it were – as distinctively, and may I say it, as *appropriately* – as when he lived as a Palestinian Jew in the early first century.

Andrew Walls

Mission is the Feast of the Epiphany celebrated on a global scale.

David Bosch

Good missiology is made at the kitchen table. Meaningful missiology is made in the context of relationship. . . . Relationship-building is an essential part of our journey towards tomorrow.

Valdir Steuernagel

One of the biggest barriers to cross-cultural mission within countries is that of prejudice and hostility between neighbouring but different groups.

Kang San Tan

Is the gospel always the same when it crosses frontiers?

Perhaps you might respond, "Of course! The gospel is always the same gospel!" And, at one level that is absolutely right. The Good News about who Jesus is, and what he has done, is unchanged and unchangeable. From before time began, through time, and into boundless eternity, the Lord Jesus is "the same, yesterday, today and forever". That's glorious, and we are right to rejoice in it! Further, the fact of human fallenness, and the need to be rescued, is universal. In fact, all the fundamentals of the Christian faith are true in every generation and for every human being, whether or not we choose to acknowledge them and take shelter beneath them. Who we are, where we are, and when we are, can't change what Francis Schaeffer graphically called "true truth".

Yet, as the early church very swiftly discovered, *how you present the message* and *what godly discipleship looks like* may be quite dramatically different in different cultures and settings. Actually, even a brief study of the Gospels soon shows that the Lord Jesus himself approached different people in very different ways. He told Nicodemus, the religious expert, that he needed to set all that expertise on one side, humbly go back to the beginning all over again like a newborn baby, and start out on a new Spirit-birthed life. He told the long-term cripple at the Pool of Bethesda that he must get up and walk. He told the man lowered through the roof by his friends that his sins were forgiven – and that (in this case) the evidence was that he could walk away physically healed as well. He told the rich young ruler that he must give away all his wealth. He instructed a man delivered from many demons to go and tell everybody what

God had done for him, but the friends of a healed deaf-mute not to tell anybody. Salvation, and the coming of the kingdom of God, engaged meaningfully with different people in different ways. The reality behind it was the same, but the "route in" varied.

And, not long after Pentecost, as soon as the gospel passed beyond the enclave of the Jews, the Apostles found themselves grappling with some profound questions. Which bits of Jewish heritage were intrinsic to the gospel, and which were simply the way Jews liked to do things? After Peter's seismic encounter with Cornelius, the church digests the fact that "God has granted even the Gentiles repentance unto life" (Acts 11:18). Yet, years later at the Council of Jerusalem, they are still struggling with the implications. It takes the combined weight of Peter and James, Paul and Barnabas, to persuade everybody that Gentiles should not be required to be circumcised – that is, become Jews in order to become Christians. Rightly, they see that this is a crucial issue which goes to the very heart of the meaning of salvation. They cannot compromise on it.

It is hard to overstate the importance of this momentous Council. Nor should we dismiss the "Judaisers" as foolish or obstinate or somehow not truly committed to Jesus. In many respects, Jewish culture had been so deeply formed by God's revelation that it was natural for Jewish Christians to assume that there would be significant continuity in expressing devotion to God, that is, living out a daily life of discipleship in concrete terms. Nonetheless, the Judaisers were critically mistaken. But, following the Council, it is intriguing to trace the ways in which the apostles varied their message (compare, for example, the content of the different sermons in Acts) or addressed different concerns in the Epistles.

As it happens, there have been parallel questions facing God's people wherever the church has crossed new cultural boundaries. For example, for many centuries the Roman

Catholic Church tried to ensure uniformity by having the same structures throughout its territories, by deciding doctrine and practice centrally in Rome, by using the same rites in the same language (Latin), and by prescribing one pattern for all. It is perhaps easy for those of other traditions to assume this was all about power (which it wasn't necessarily or for all leaders) and to miss the obvious attractiveness of being able to move about and always find a familiar form of the Faith.

Nonetheless, generally, when clergy tried to translate the Bible into the local language, for example, or missionaries deviated from standard norms, they were speedily and often ruthlessly dealt with. But, there were always those who worked hard to adapt what they did and how they did it to fit a new context. However, if you came supported by military power and imposed conversion on people, of course you did not need to make any adjustments. Whether what you did and said really changed people deep down was another matter. But, if you came in weakness and vulnerability, the story could be rather different. It concentrated your mind to find ways to build genuine bridges for the gospel, so that voluntarily people would want to become disciples of Jesus within the specific realities of their setting.

The Protestant modern missionary movement has had a rather mixed record. On the one hand, there were inevitably some who rode in on the back of one imperial expansion or another, and for them, too, it was fatally easy to articulate the Faith and train people to live just like Christians back home. For others, the issue was genuinely not one of power and deliberate high-handed imposition so much as a sheer lack of imagination, or possibly an unquestioned assumption that homeside culture was Christian culture and therefore "the way we do it back home" must be universal and transferable. Or it could be that with terribly brief life expectancy – for example in West Africa, graphically nicknamed "the White Man's Grave" – most missionary pioneers didn't have time to learn language and culture, or certainly not at leisure, before they died. That they communicated the gospel at all, and that churches came into being at all, is truly a miracle of God's grace.

It is easy, and unfair, simply to point to some of the absurdities of what happened: Nigerians feeling they could not celebrate communion properly unless resplendent in frock coat and waistcoat, for thus had the Europeans come; congregations in tropical heat singing Christmas carols about snow and winter; church buildings in India that could have been lifted straight out of some Victorian industrial city. Sad though these things are, they were certainly no more inappropriate than most other things done by the missionaries' business and colonial counterparts. Interestingly enough, many of the new wave of missionaries from the two-thirds world, who may have been sensitive to the cultural imperialism of missionaries in their own countries, are now repeating the same pattern. It may be harder than one might think to disentangle one's cultural trappings from biblical truth. The fact is that the only way in which we can live our lives is within the three-dimensional context of culture, so we are all accustomed to expressing our Christian faith in concrete cultural forms. We can't help it.

The gospel in its setting: the Incarnation applied

During the second half of the twentieth century, there was a great deal of reflection and debate about contextualisation. It was not entirely new. As early as 1841, Henry Venn, newly appointed secretary of the Church Missionary Society, was arguing cogently for the need for mission churches to become as soon as possible absolutely self-supporting (no outside financial help), self-governing (leadership entirely in the hands of national believers), and self-propagating (taking responsibility for multiplying congregations themselves). This came to be known as *the indigenous principle*. If the gospel was to make significant progress in new settings, then it must become indigenous (i.e. natural to the context) rather than foreign. After all, this was the principle of the incarnation of the Lord Jesus: one of the chief reasons why he became human was so that he might display what God is like in terms human beings could comprehend.

At different times, other missionary statesmen articulated similar principles, and indeed many missionaries worked hard to practise them. There are numerous lovely examples of enormous mutual respect between missionary and national Christians. But the rise of high imperialism in the late nineteenth century, and evolutionary assumptions in the same period and later, made it all too easy for some Westerners to treat Africans and Asians as children not yet adult enough to control their own affairs. In some cases, denominational missions inevitably brought their churches under the over-arching structure of the parent body, located in Europe or North America, and that made it impossible to implement the "Three Self" concept properly. In yet other contexts, the national believers preferred to live in a measure of dependency on foreigners, and themselves strongly resisted taking responsibility for their own affairs.

But, from the middle of the twentieth century, as colonies became independent, Henry Venn's prophetic wisdom became increasingly apparent. The churches that were most indigenous were on the whole the ones that were best able to survive the upheavals, political and economic, that tended to accompany independence. This was both because they were perceived as "belonging to us" rather than to the foreigners from whom nationals were trying to distance themselves, and also because they were not dependent on foreign personnel and foreign funds, both of which were often now cut off. In fact, the more indigenous the church, the more likely it was to be at the forefront of the movement for political independence. And, in the final quarter of the twentieth century, a vast number of indigenous churches and denominations have sprung up all over the world. These vary enormously, from those expressing their Christian faith in healthy, biblical and contextualised ways, to the frankly syncretistic – that is, incorporating so much local culture as to be no longer authentically Christian in some crucial areas. It would be a mistake to think that this is only a problem in Africa or Asia. There are churches in Europe and North America which have so incorporated cultural values of wealth, success and entertainment (for example) as to be very far removed from the teaching of Christ or of the Apostles. Implicitly or explicitly, such gospel fundamentals as the atoning death of the Lord Jesus Christ, the reality of human sinfulness and the need of rescue by the Saviour, may be denied, and Christian discipleship reduced to therapeutic self-fulfilment.

Critical contextualisation: relevance and faithfulness combined

In recent decades, there has been extensive heart-searching about context and contextualisation. There are, of course, still those who believe that even to contemplate contextualisation is to sell out to the spirit of the age, and that it must automatically lead to syncretism and unfaithfulness. For them, the *form* of Christian discipleship, and the *formulation* of the Christian faith, must always remain the same, whatever the context, whatever the culture, whatever the generation. This, sadly, has contributed to the decline or even demise of effective Christian testimony in some parts of Europe. The expression of Christian truth and worship, and the way of life of believers, no longer engages in any meaningful way at all with the unbelieving community. It is caught in an archaic time-warp. There may be an entirely praiseworthy anxiety to be biblically faithful (which is vitally important) or simply an inability to face change in any shape or form (which is spiritual suicide).

At the other extreme, for some there has been such a concern to be relevant and contemporary that far too much has been conceded. Because the gospel always challenges us at every level – culturally, intellectually, morally, for example – contextualisation should never be confused with comfort. The Lord Jesus' claims will always disturb our comfort and urge upon us the usually *uncomfortable*, even painful, reality of progressive transformation.

No, the answer is neither to ignore context and culture (and thus be largely irrelevant), nor on the other hand to embrace context and culture without discernment (and thus drift into syncretism). Rather, what is needed is what has come to be called *critical contextualisation*. This combines a rightful recognition of the need to be relevant, and the need to remove unnecessary cultural barriers to the gospel, with a passionate concern to be faithful to God's truth. God's truth is unchanging, but the way in which it is understood and applied may differ in a changing world.

Some have concluded that the best thing for Christians to do is in the simplest way possible to "tell the story" and "live the story" of Jesus Christ, leaving the Holy Spirit to shape an emerging church however he wills. On the one hand, undoubtedly we need to tell and live the story. But, on the other, as the Epistles graphically illustrate, further explanation and corrective is also needed. That is why all believers everywhere need the whole Bible and not just parts of it. And, even then, without some appreciation of cultural contexts of different parts of the Bible, and of the way these differ from our own, we may miss, or misunderstand, the meaning of God's message.

How important, then, that we grapple with issues of contextualisation! This, surely, is part of loving the Lord with our total personalities, and our neighbours as ourselves.

In the next chapter, we shall look briefly at some areas which illustrate the need for critical contextualisation today.

Questions

1. Think of someone of a different ethnic background from your own. What elements of his or her culture would you need to take into account when trying to explain the story of Jesus?

2. Invite a Christian from a culture other than your own (perhaps an overseas student) to explain to you the things which he found strange when he came to your country. In particular, what are the things he has found different in the way Christians live and worship?

3. How can we distinguish between some non-negotiable aspect of God's revelation and the cultural form in which we are accustomed to expressing it?

4. In what ways could we apply "the indigenous principle" to the church in our own country, especially in thinking about helping young people and children feel at home in it as "their" community?

14

More than Skin Deep

All over the world, Christians have to bear witness to Jesus
Christ in the context of cities, and of other faiths. The great
non-Christian religions are often strong and confident: how
do we relate to them, especially in a generation when many
Christians have lost their conviction that Jesus Christ
uniquely is the way to God? And, what are the special
challenges and opportunities posed by postmodernity?

More than Skin Deep

It is my contention that in the encounter with people of other religious persuasions or no religious persuasion, Christians should confess openly their missionary identity. It belongs to the centre of our faith, to our understanding of God. It is basic to our Christology and to our anthropology.

Emilio Castro

According to a recent Gallup poll . . . some 52% of American adults believe that all good people will go to heaven, regardless of their beliefs. Even 45% of those Americans classified as born-again Christians say a person can earn a place in heaven through good works.

Stan Guthrie

William Carey, Hudson Taylor, and the founder of every mission in the IFMA [Interdenominational Foreign Mission Association of America] shared a common conviction that personal faith in Jesus Christ is the only way of salvation for all people everywhere and that those who die without this saving knowledge face eternal damnation.

John Orme

Today the number of people living in cities outnumbers the entire population of the world 150 years ago.

John Palen

Have you ever tried to explain the sheep and shepherd images of the Bible to people who have no pastoral way of life in their culture at all? Or the fact of the one and only true and living God to a people who have ten million gods and still counting? The love of God in a culture where there is no word for love in the language? Eternal life to someone who can only think in terms of reincarnation? Faithfulness to someone who has only ever experienced desertion and betrayal? Yet, the amazing fact is that there will be people from all these backgrounds and every other you could ever find, drawn by the love of God and by the power of the Spirit into radically new life in the Lord Jesus, amongst that unnumbered throng in heaven. Being a disciple, making disciples, is not something impossible, something God dangles in front of us to taunt us with. It's on his heart, and the Cross and resurrection of the Lord Jesus is the guarantee that he keeps his promises.

What's beneath *your* skin?

One of the reasons why critical contextualisation is so important is that where it is ignored, Christian discipleship is frequently very superficial: only skin deep. If the gospel does not engage at a deep level with the daily realities of believers' lives, they may be "Sunday Christians", that is, going to church on a Sunday and taking part in some of the outward life of the church, but not integrating their Christian faith in their home life, their work life and their community life. This leads to a form of spiritual schizophrenia, which sooner or later leads either to nominalism or to outright apostasy (turning one's back on one's faith and going back to pre-Christian ways).

There is an urgent need to deal with real and specific issues in each culture: this is the level where conversion and change must take place for the gospel to have credibility and genuine engagement in that setting. The details may well be different from place to place, community to community, even individual to individual.

For example, how could it be that in Rwanda, only a generation earlier swept by extensive revival, there should then come one of the most tragic outbursts of ethnic hatred in a blood-stained century? It was not that the revival was not genuine. There is plenty of evidence that it was genuinely a work of the Holy Spirit, even if inevitably there was also some counterfeit mixed up with it. The problem seems to be that the teaching and application that accompanied it tended to focus on very limited areas of reconciliation and dealing with sin. It dealt (powerfully) with matters of personal reconciliation with God, with domestic and family reconciliation, and the need for forgiveness between church members (usually of the same tribal background). But, in particular, it did not adequately and insistently enough address the deep-level tribal hatred. Many Christians who had experienced the revival still did not necessarily have any experience of living in true harmony and at close quarters with those across the ethnic divide. When conflict came, the hatred came bubbling up to the surface again.

In the Balkans, or Sri Lanka, or Indonesia, or Ireland, it is not possible today to have an authentic church which does not speak prophetically to the issue of ethnic hatred, and live out a message of forgiveness rather than retaliation and violence. It is, of course, desperately easy to write that, and entirely different to be those who suffer, even to the point of martyrdom. Yet, in that context, gospel life demands it.

In much of Africa and Asia, critical contextualisation must address issues that are unfamiliar in the Western world, and which by and large do not figure in our theological and pastoral textbooks: relating to the ancestors, polygamy, every kind of spirit practice, female circumcision, killing girl babies or twins, widespread poverty and disease. In much of Europe and North America, critical contextualisation must address issues of rampant capitalism, individualism, greed, addiction to pleasure, exploitation, abuse of power, promiscuity. These are not even issues, any of them, found solely in the surrounding non-Christian culture. They are issues that dog the lives of those inside the church, too. The world is in the church.

Culture is not neutral, and in its susceptibility to sin it too readily squeezes us into the world's mould rather than assisting us in our growth as disciples. At the same time, culture is the vehicle through which we live in practice rather than in theory, and Christians have the exciting potential to be active rather than passive in demonstrating a different way of living. What's under your skin, and mine?

Babel – modern (skyscraper) style

One of the most significant and far-reaching changes of the past century has been the rate of urbanisation, that is, the phenomenal pace at which the world's population has shifted from being primarily rural to being primarily city-based. Of course, there are still some countries where millions of people live in village settings, often as subsistence farmers, growing just enough food for their own needs. But, increasingly the world's people are found packed into cities.

This is of immense significance when we think about world mission today, because cities are different sociologically and culturally from rural areas. By and large, cities are more impersonal, more violent, more isolating, than many village communities. The greater majority of the world's very poor and destitute live in the slums and ghettos and gutters of our cities. The drainage to the cities breaks up families and weakens the glue of traditional cultures. It destroys hope, and breeds extremism born of despair. Of course, there are good things that happen in cities, too, usually for those with power or money or education. But for most of the world's newly urban people, it is the negative that far outweighs the positive. The poverty of the countryside is compounded in the city by pollution and every kind of concentrated sin.

Even in the affluent West, where cities may be more friendly places to a higher proportion of the population, and where urbanisation has happened more gradually and over a longer period, Christians are still struggling to find appropriate ways of discipleship at the communal level. Suburban churches may flourish, but truly urban ones mostly do not.

There is not space here to explore this, but it is an area where we need to give deep thought to issues of contextualisation – and, indeed, there are some exciting experiments already under way in some cities. For most of its history, the church has been operating in a largely rural, or small town, world. Such cities as there have been have borne little resemblance to today's with their teeming, jam-packed millions. Further, the world(s) of the Old and New Testaments are primarily rural, or small town. Even Jerusalem or Rome, by today's standards, would rank merely as largish towns. So, naturally, the biblical message is embedded in the language and life and images of the countryside: shepherds and sheep, fishermen in small craft, the village well, communities where people are recognised and known by name.

If we simply "tell the story" in those terms, much of it is a world apart from how most people live today. Without losing the essential thread of the story, we need to be able not only to tell it as it is but also to translate it – faithfully and relevantly – into the language of cities. The call to discipleship comes to us in the here and now of our real lives, not in some sanitised rural idyll after which we nostalgically hanker (which isn't what rural life is about anyway). This is critical contextualisation at work.

They're happy as they are

The twentieth century transformed the worldwide church, not least because in the course of one century the Christian Faith truly became a world faith. Today the majority of the world's professing Christians are to be found outside Europe and North America.

Nonetheless, it remains painfully true that the majority of those who have come to faith have done so from a background of animism rather than from committed Islam, Buddhism,

Hinduism or other major world religions. The Islamic, Buddhist and Hindu worlds remain largely "uncracked"; and, since these are areas where population growth tends to be at its most explosive, the overall percentage of professing Christians in global terms is dropping slightly.

The Western church, and therefore much of the modern missionary movement, was not very well equipped to deal well with other religions. Until the last fifty years, you could live all your life in the familiar environment of Christendom and never meet a practising Muslim or Hindu or Buddhist. Of course, there were those who thought and wrote perceptively about alien cultures and religions, which they sought respectfully and carefully to understand. And there were some who tried to find culturally appropriate ways of expressing their Christian faith, both by word and by life. But rather few grappled with the deep questions posed by other religions. Islam, Hinduism and Buddhism have all seen their own renewal movements in recent decades, sometimes linked to fundamentalist movements, and have become more confident than they often were in the nineteenth century. This, together with issues of nationalism, resentment of Western political and economic manipulation, and distaste for Western moral decadence, has made it increasingly difficult to engage in mission among some people groups.

At the same time, the decline of the church in the West combined with much greater exposure to those of other faiths has too often led to pluralism, that is, the belief that different religions are simply varied but equally valid ways to God. Ironically, of course, neither Islam, Judaism nor Buddhism – for different reasons – permits the concept of pluralism, even though some adherents of all these faiths may personally embrace it. Hinduism alone of the great world religions can cope comfortably with pluralism. It is only by abandoning certain core beliefs of Christianity, Islam or Judaism, that one can accommodate pluralism. Sadly, some "Christian" theologians have been at the forefront of the movement to popularise it and to give it widespread respectability.

No Christian who takes the Great Commission seriously can simultaneously subscribe to pluralism. All authority, for time and eternity, is vested in the Lord Jesus Christ, and in him specifically. While we humbly need to admit that we do not have all the answers to every question about how God will deal with those who have never heard the gospel, the Bible simply does not permit us to see salvation as possible through any other means than the sacrificial death of the one and only Son of God, Jesus Christ.

There has been a steady erosion of confidence in the uniqueness of Christ even in some evangelical churches. This has led to pressure to focus on relief, development and compassion ministries (all of which are of course essential areas of proper Christian concern), and embarrassment over overt evangelism or church planting (especially among those of other faiths). It is now easier to raise money to bore a well or build a new school than it is to support a church planter or Bible translator. Further, in the interests of "political correctness", there are now places – for instance, many British university campuses – where a Muslim may be free to propagate his beliefs publicly but an evangelical Christian is not.

So there is an urgent need to think afresh about how we should regard other religions, and how practically we live and bear witness to Jesus Christ among them. What kind of apologetics (defence and explanation of the gospel in a hostile environment) is appropriate? How can we build bridges for the gospel in this specific setting or that? And, when people do become Christians, how shall we then disciple them? Liverpool isn't Lagos isn't Lahore.

All change in the West

Culture may not be neutral, but neither is it static. And, in the

West, many observers believe we are entering a period of cultural change quite as major as that of the Reformation, or of the Industrial Revolution. Further, while this phenomenon, known as postmodernity, at the moment most deeply impacts the West, it would be a mistake to think that that's all there is to it. The mass media guarantee not only global impact, but also a more rapid culture shift than perhaps any comparable change of the past.

As with all contexts, postmodernity paradoxically offers both roadblocks and doorways for the gospel. Among the roadblocks – barriers to the gospel – there is rejection of the very idea that there is absolute truth, and certainly that any ultimate truth is knowable. Reality is fragmented and individualised. The past may have brought us to the present, but it has nothing to say of value for the present – or for the future (if there is a future). Human experience can only be of alienation and despair, so one might as well live selfishly. We all have our own personal story (or stories), but it is impossible to believe that any one story (in this case, the biblical narrative) is of any special significance – certainly not significance to the whole human race. Words are unreliable – they only mean what they mean to a particular listener or reader, and even she might understand them differently tomorrow from today, or if he is wearing blue instead of green. The only thing that matters is now's experience, now's buzz, now's pleasure. No-one shall tell me what to do or not to do.

All of these and more have profound significance. Each of them makes it harder for an unbeliever to come to faith in Jesus Christ, and, as these various "values" become increasingly deeply embedded in our culture(s), they will shape people at both conscious and subconscious levels. So, not only in the initial stages of turning from unbelief to faith but also all along the way in ongoing discipleship, there will be important areas of thought and life to be challenged and remade.

Yet, we should not despair! There are also elements of

postmodernity which clear away some of the debris of the past few centuries (for example, the growing pride in human achievement and the power of reason), and others which offer "ways in", different though these may be from "ways in" in the past. So, postmodernity encourages people to pursue spirituality (fuzzy and pluralistic though that sense of spirituality may be). It encourages people to see rationality as inadequate, and to look for meaning in relationships (and what relationship could be more meaningful than relationship with God?). It encourages people to search the unfamiliar (and authentic Christianity may well be unfamiliar to the majority of Europeans), to hunger for a community to give identity (and the church is called to be the community within which we develop our profoundest identity as God's children). It encourages people to question the status quo (and for at least a generation that status quo has ridiculed and marginalised Christian faith).

These are exciting days in which to be Great Commission disciples within this pulsing, changing, weary, unfulfilled Western world! How much we need the wisdom and discernment that come from God to be effective, faithful, communicating, empowered disciples in our context.

Questions

1. In your own culture, what do you see as the major obstacles to people becoming disciples of Jesus Christ? What parts of your culture make it hardest for Christians to grow in their faith?

2. In your own culture, what do you see as the most effective bridges for the gospel, to arrest the attention of unbelievers? What parts of your culture encourage Christians to grow in their faith?

3. How might you take the picture of Jesus as the Good Shepherd, or the story of the Prodigal Son, and retell them

to communicate with someone who has never been outside his city?

4. How would you set about explaining the uniqueness of Jesus Christ as the only way to God to a devout Muslim or Hindu friend?

15

Getting on with the Job

Carey provoked Christians to think in two crucial ways: first, to think globally (God is concerned for the whole world, and this is what it looks like), and, second, to think strategically (*how* should we set about discipling all the nations?) These two themes – thinking globally, and thinking strategically – are still as contemporary for us as they were two hundred years ago for Carey, though today Christians from all around the world share in the response.

Getting on with the Job

We have come through an extended time of institutionalisation. We felt that we could organise and manage our way to world evangelisation. The natural laws that seem to control the rest of institutional life seem to shape us as well.

Paul McKaughan

The third millennium may bring us back to a situation reminiscent of the early church, where our mission will necessarily be from weakness, foolishness, and poverty.

Charles Van Engen

There can be no hierarchy of vocations, for God's estimate of the value of life's service is not determined by the geographical position in which that service is rendered; rather it is determined by the extent to which it is according to His will.

David Adeney

When I came to England I met a certain saint of God. We talked about the revival in China, and she gave me certain dates when God specially pressed her to pray. I was almost startled on looking up those dates to find that they were the very dates when God was doing His mightiest work in Manchuria and China.

Jonathan Goforth (1859–1936)

Here then we see God's way of success in our work – a trinity of prayer, faith and patience.

JO Fraser (1886–1938)

Now to him who is able to do immeasurably more than all we ask or imagine, according to his power that is at work within us, to him be the glory in the church and in Christ Jesus throughout all generations, for ever and ever! Amen.

Ephesians 3:20–21

"What," I asked an African brother, "helped you most become a disciple of the Lord Jesus, and then keep going?"

"Well," he said, "I realised that Jesus is the most powerful of all beings, far more powerful than the spirits, and that because he died for me I could come under his protection now and for ever. I saw the Holy Spirit changing people, and at work through Christians. And a friend kept patiently telling me and my family about what the Bible says. He didn't just tell us. It was the way he lived. So I thought, I want to live like this, too."

And I thought, that sounds to me just like the Great Commission!

If William Carey, that intrepid pioneer who set off for India in 1793, were to come back to today's world, his eyes would pop out of his head. On the one hand, much of the world (though not quite all of it) has been changed beyond recognition. On the other, the church, too, has changed beyond recognition, crossing geographical and cultural frontiers on every continent and becoming a kaleidoscope of colours and ethnic groups and denominations.

The year before he left the soft familiarity of England, Carey published his brief, cumbersomely titled book, *An Enquiry into the Obligation of Christians to use Means for the Conversion of the Heathen*. It was dynamite, even if some of the explosions took a while coming. The burden of it was not only that Christians *must* be committed to the Great Commission, but that they needed to adopt properly thought-out strategies as to *how* it might be accomplished.

Others before him had of course consciously or unconsciously addressed that question, too, as they struggled to find ways of making Christian faith meaningful to others around them. But for the most part, as we saw in Part 2, it was in a limited geographical setting. As far as we know, nobody had done what Carey now did: assemble data for the whole world in order to get a complete global overview. What was the population in this country or that, on that continent or that? How many Christians were there? What other religions were there? How many followers did they have? Here was the true precursor to Patrick Johnstone's twentieth century goldmine, *Operation World*.

Carey's information was rudimentary, but it is astonishing that he should have gathered it at all. It is an amazing testimony to a prodigious intellect. But Carey was also influenced by the philosophical mindset of his generation, with its enormous energy and the growing confidence that any problem could be mastered by human prowess provided one broke it down into manageable steps. This was how steam was harnessed to transform machinery, for example. Observe, collect data, establish what you want to achieve, experiment (confidently!) until you achieve it.

Carey thus (perhaps unconsciously) changed the way people thought about the Great Commission in two critical ways: comprehensiveness and strategy. Carey thought of the world as a coherent whole. However crude the leather map he made to hang over his cobbler's bench, there were no significant omissions. He spurred Christians to think *globally*. But he also implicitly assumed that the whole world *could* be evangelised, *should* be evangelised, and that "the task" was capable of completion. It was, he suggested, the responsibility of the church to set about it systematically: if Christ's mandate was to go into the whole world, it should be demonstrable that that was indeed what Christians were obeying.

In a variety of ways, these two themes are woven throughout the two centuries of the modern missionary movement. They have not always meant the same thing to different people, but the themes are traceable. Carey himself was a deeply Reformed man, from a strict Baptist background. That shaped how he thought about these basic ideas. For him, everything was embraced within the over-arching truth of the sovereignty of God, and that affected in particular how he thought about strategy. Human responsibility must be active, not passive, but always with great humility deferring to God's sovereign right to over-rule creaturely planning. Others since have come from different theological frameworks, and that in turn has coloured their understanding. Some have so stressed divine sovereignty as to leave rather little room for human planning, while others again have gone to the opposite extreme, devising detailed plans and appearing to expect God to be obliged to fall in with them without demur.

Thinking globally

In Part 2, we saw how at different times Roman Catholic, Orthodox, Protestant and Pentecostal expansion took place. Usually, these followed trade routes, emigration patterns, or the expansion of empires. Very practical considerations came into play, too. You went where you had heard about. You went where you could plod on foot (maybe even for many hundreds of miles), or where you could travel by sea. And, if you were going to survive at all, you probably wouldn't go far inland on the great continents, where wild animals, deadly disease, and cannibals were waiting to pounce upon strange white men. Because, for quite a while, it really was "white men" (and, more and more, white women!): from the West, to the rest.

Through the nineteenth century, that pattern quietly but steadily began to change. Carey, and many another, trained national evangelists and Bible women, and soon in India, Africa, Latin America and Asia there was a growing army of native disciples who themselves were dedicated disciple-makers. They are frequently unsung and unacknowledged, but as one scours early records and reports and letters one quickly realises how many of them there must have been. Further, during the second half of the century, thanks to the vision and determination of pioneers such as Livingstone in Africa and Hudson Taylor in China, the gospel was being taken far inland.

During the twentieth century, globalisation accelerated phenomenally, driven in large measure by the transformation of communication and travel, and the increasingly complex inter-locking of the world economy. The world church became multinational on a scale undreamed of such a short time before, and more and more found itself caught up in the frenetic movement of people around the globe. For the church, as for everyone else, this was no longer a context of "from the West, to the rest" but "from everywhere to everywhere".

Travel is far easier, speedier and cheaper than it has ever been, and, as far as we can tell, there are very few places in the world that are genuinely inaccessible to all Christians from absolutely anywhere. That is not the same as saying that all Christians can go anywhere. For instance, probably as many as 80 per cent of East Asians live in countries which do not permit expatriate missionary work, and in some cases Westerners in particular are very unwelcome. But, for example, sometimes Nigerians or Koreans or Brazilians can go where Americans or Britons may not, or in one way or another exposure to the gospel may be possible. In many countries there is exciting cross-cultural mission being undertaken by nationals who have the right of movement even though foreigners may not go there. In other places, while overt missionary activity is forbidden, Christians quietly and faithfully live out the life of the disciple and disciple-maker as they contribute a valued professional skill or engage in business.

In recent decades, Carey's broad brush stroke data has been greatly refined, and we can see where the most neglected areas of the world are. Once, these were large, and usually (very understandably) geographically defined. Now, in our highly mobile world, these may be "people groups" still to be found in one place or perhaps scattered across political boundaries –

which do not always follow cultural and linguistic boundaries very accurately anyway.

On the one hand, thinking globally for us means taking stock of the whole world, and we have unprecedented opportunity to do that. On the other, it includes thinking carefully and prayerfully about the most effective ways of reaching "unreached" sub-groups, and recognising the separate segments within the whole. It means finding ways and means of mobilising Christian disciples from everywhere to cross frontiers into the world of unbelief wherever it may be found, close at hand or far away. It means thinking creatively about establishing a witness to the Lord Jesus Christ in those communities where as yet there is no indigenous church. It means having the whole people of God, from wherever, joining hands to respond to the Great Commission as a whole-family calling.

This means in turn that the model of the missionary society, which served well as a dominant model for two centuries, will probably need radical (and painful) adaptation to meet the needs of a new context. That model grew out of the West, and in structure and organisation, as well as economically, may not be readily transferable elsewhere. There is something very powerful in the witness of an international missionary community working well and harmoniously together, particularly where either so far there is no church at all, or where, in the context of an emerging or established national church there is godly humble service under national leadership. There remain places where "traditional" missionary societies still have a crucial role to play.

But, in the poorer economies of some parts of Africa and Asia, national Christians are gradually working out much simpler patterns of crossing frontiers, perhaps sending a couple of families to live in a new district not far away, or following unbelieving relatives who have moved to another town or city. In many Western countries, there are large numbers of immigrants, or temporary residents and students, from countries where the church may be small or besieged: how shall we seek to make disciples among these?

The Apostle John recorded for us his beautiful vision of those from every corner of the globe worshipping together in heaven, around the throne of the Lamb. Living in today's world, with images from every continent flashing across our TV screens every day, it is more possible than ever before to anticipate how glorious a gathering that will be. Thinking globally is an inspiration, not a burden!

Thinking methodologically

One of the most critical issues of all relating to mission practice today, and one which has provoked extensive (sometimes acrimonious) debate, is related to the way in which we draw on the behavioural sciences – sociology, anthropology, psychology, management theory, among others.

The "can do" confidence in human prowess of Carey's day, coupled with popularised evolutionary theory, led naturally by the beginning of the twentieth century to a growing number of new academic and theoretical disciplines related to human behaviour. Because of the time at which they emerged, and the context from which they emerged, they are almost all post-Christian disciplines; that is, their fundamental philosophical framework is shaped by secular humanism, not Christian faith. While some would claim that this provides neutrality and objectivity, that is clearly not the case. True and objective truth is inseparably tied to the reality of God – his character, his statements about purpose and design, his revelation about human character and the nature of society.

These very fundamental truths provide the lens through which we observe the world, and, even more crucially, through which we interpret what we observe. In so far as the behavioural sciences diverge at this foundational level from what God says is the fact of the matter, so far will they be distorted in their findings and conclusions. In relation to the practice of mission, this is clearly of the utmost significance, because here we are dealing at profound levels with the truth about human nature, about what community is designed by the Creator to look like, and about what constitutes healthy living. The most important things that can be said about human nature – that we are created in the image of God, that we are fallen and in need of being redeemed and changed, that we have divinely ordained destination and purpose, the basis on which we are to live together – all these and many more are excluded from or explicitly denied by the literature and prevailing ideas of the behavioural sciences.

It is therefore of absolutely crucial importance that what we use from the behavioural sciences is most carefully sieved through the grid of biblical truth. It is biblical truth above all else which must shape our planning and strategising and doing and being, for the church, for mission, for leadership formation. This has immense implications for Great Commission Christians today. Recent decades have seen numerous programmes launched and methods urged, sometimes with the claim behind them that if we do it *this* way, or break the greater task down into these manageable smaller tasks, then successful completion of world evangelisation may be confidently predicted. Sometimes even a timeframe is supplied: do it like this, and in five years, or ten years, or two years, the Lord can come back, because everybody will have "heard the gospel".

As we saw in Part 1, there is no biblical encouragement to think in these terms. There is no suggestion even that we can ever say that a person or community is "fully evangelised", let alone fully discipled. That is a process which will always be continuous *until the time when the Lord sovereignly determines to return*. We are explicitly told that we shall not know that date in advance. No programme can *guarantee* "success", no technique can "bind Satan", no timetable can be dictated to God. If there is true growth in the church, in numbers and in godliness, if there is real advance, if men and women and children are being born anew, this is the work of grace of our sovereign Lord – and we had better not forget that. Yes, he invites us into real partnership with him as disciples, and, walking with him in love and obedience, we have a task to engage in. But the Spirit blows as he wills, not as we direct. Out of love, the disciple will be content to do his part, neither more nor less, and trust God to do what only he can do, in his own way and in his own time.

That does not mean that we have nothing valuable to learn from the behavioural sciences (and certainly from humble faith-filled planning). Provided that we are alert and thorough in our scrutiny, appropriately critical in our evaluation, we may find many helpful tools. In recent decades, world mission has greatly benefited, for example, from insights from cultural anthropology, enabling us to look with greater understanding at diverse cultures and how people function in them. We have benefited from linguistics, and been able to learn unfamiliar languages more fluently and translate Scripture more accurately. We have benefited from statistical data.

Further, without a doubt, many of those who have most passionately drawn on the behavioural sciences have done so precisely because of their enormous longing to see people all over the world, from every nook and cranny of humanity, brought to faith in Jesus Christ. Their enthusiasm for the gospel is beyond question. Whether or not we feel able to adopt their methods and strategies, we must deeply respect their whole-hearted commitment.

Yet, we need once again to remember that God calls us to engage in world mission not out of human confidence, but out of weakness and vulnerability, dependent not on what we design but on what God mercifully does. This is a hard lesson for Western Christians in particular to learn. Our cultures are very confident, very proud. Perhaps the Lord must humble us very painfully to make us understand that we cannot achieve genuinely spiritual goals through human effort.

The Lord Jesus once said to his friends, "I came not to be served, but to serve and to give my life as a ransom for many". In Philippians chapter 2, the magnificent early church hymn quoted by the Apostle Paul is prefaced by these words: "Your attitude should be the same as that of Christ Jesus". Then the hymn invites us to worship and wonder as we sing of the One who as Lord of the universe becomes the servant of a fallen world of sinners, pouring out his life, embracing unmerited death, for sheer love. Well, says Paul, that's how we are to live as disciples, too.

As we look forward, there are many things we do not and cannot know: we do not know when the Lord will return, we do not know when time will come to an end, we do not know all the ways in which men and women will be brought to faith. But this we know, that as long as time and our world endures, the Lord's command to his people remains: as we go, wherever we go, we are to be, and make, disciples, under his authority which transcends all others, and in the constant company of the Holy Spirit.

Questions

1. How may data and information help us engage responsibly in world mission today?

2. In what ways can we be committed to world mission globally (that is, with concern for the whole world) and in what ways can we focus our commitment in a much more specific manner? What factors might help us identify our own personal role, or that of our local church?

3. How do God's sovereignty and human responsibility balance each other in relation to the Great Commission? How can we "use means" appropriately without losing

sight of the fact that spiritual life and growth is a work of God?

4. At the end of this book, are there responses or commitments you need to make?

Further reading

If you would like to read some more about some of the themes of this book, here are some ideas.

The Lion Handbook, *The History of Christianity,* is a marvellous goldmine to help you trace the story of the church from the beginning to the present. It is designed to dip into, with short articles, and plenty of illustrations. It is edited by Tim Dowley, pub. Lion, 1990 (revised edition).

For many people, reading biographies is a good way to trace the story. There are plenty!

I Believe in Mission by Alistair Brown, pub. Hodder, 1997
Changing the Mind of Missions by James Engel & William Dyrness, pub. IVP, 2000
Missions in the Third Millennium by Stan Guthrie, pub. Paternoster, 2000
Operation World by Patrick Johnstone, pub. OM Publishing, 2001
We are the World by David Lundy, pub. OM Publishing, 1999
Let the Nations be Glad by John Piper, pub. IVP, 1993

Then, three slightly more demanding books:

Changing Frontiers of Mission by Wilbert Shenk, pub. Orbis, 1999

The Bible and the Flag by Brian Stanley, pub. IVP/Apollos, 1990

Evangelical Faith and Public Zeal ed. by John Wolffe, pub. SPCK, 1995

English-speaking OMF centres

AUSTRALIA: PO Box 849, Epping, NSW 2121
Freecall 1800 227 154 E-mail: omf-australia@omf.net
www.omf.org

CANADA: 5759 Coopers Avenue, Mississauga ON, L4Z 1R9
Toll free 1-888-657-8010 E-mail: omfcanada@omf.ca
www.omf.ca

HONG KONG: PO Box 70505, Kowloon Central Post Office,
Hong Kong
E-mail: hk@omf.net *www.omf.org*

MALAYSIA: 3A Jalan Nipah, off Jalan Ampang, 55000,
Kuala Lumpur
E-mail: my@omf.net *www.omf.org*

NEW ZEALAND: PO Box 10159, Dominion Road,
Auckland 1030
Tel 9-630 5778 E-mail: omfnz@omf.net *www.omf.org*

PHILIPPINES: 900 Commonwealth Avenue, Diliman, 1101
Quezon City
E-mail: ph-hc@omf.net *www.omf.org*

SINGAPORE: 2 Cluny Road, Singapore 259570
E-mail: sno@omf.net *www.omf.org*

SOUTHERN AFRICA: PO Box 3080, Pinegowrie, 2123
E-mail: za@omf.net *www.omf.org*

UK: Station Approach, Borough Green, Sevenoaks, Kent,
TN15 8BG
Tel 01732 887299 E-mail: omf@omf.org.uk *www.omf.org.uk*

USA: 10 West Dry Creek Circle, Littleton, CO 80120-4413
Toll Free 1-800-422-5330 E-mail: omf@omf.org
www.us.omf.org

OMF International Headquarters:
2 Cluny Road, Singapore 259570